National Emergency Strikes

SO-AJE-099

by
Donald E. Cullen

ILR Paperback no. 7   October 1968

New York State School of Industrial and Labor Relations,
a Statutory College of the State University of New York,
Cornell University, Ithaca, N. Y.

Price: $2.00

ORDER FROM:

*Distribution Center, New York State School of Industrial
and Labor Relations, Cornell University, Ithaca, N. Y.*

Printed in the United States of America
by the Humphrey Press of Geneva, N. Y.

Contents

Introduction

IN THE EBB OF THE GREAT WAVE
of postwar strikes in 1945–1946, a national opinion poll reported that 32 percent of Americans favored the outlawing of all strikes in the auto industry, 43 percent would have banned all telephone strikes, and 46 percent were for compulsory arbitration of labor disputes on the railroads.[1] As strike activity declined in later years, and collective bargaining became less of a novelty on the American scene, it was tempting to shrug off this postwar revulsion against strikes as a passing phase of public opinion. Yet, in the aftermath of the 116-day steel strike of 1959, a Gallup poll recorded a thumping 59 percent vote in favor of compulsory arbitration to settle *all* labor disputes that might result in nationwide strikes.[2]

If public opinion about the big strike has actually hardened in recent years, as suggested by these two polls, then the gap between popular and expert opinion on this subject is even wider today than it was twenty years ago. At that time, most impartial experts, as well as union leaders, opposed placing any severe restrictions on the strike, stressing its importance to effective bargaining and arguing that most strike emergencies existed only in the imagination of headline writers. And since management wanted no part of compulsory arbitration, a pos-

---

[1]"The Fortune Survey," *Fortune,* vol. 34, no. 5 (November 1946), pp. 10 and 14.

[2]George Gallup, "New Laws on Strikes Favored," *Los Angeles Times,* Dec. 4, 1959, p. 31.

sible substitute for the strike, most employer spokesmen also avoided a frontal attack upon strikes in the mid-1940's, urging instead that the effects of work stoppages be limited by methods such as breaking up industry-wide bargaining.

Today, the consensus of expert opinion remains much the same: the emergency strike problem is vastly overrated by the public. Consider, for example, the following excerpts from a 1962 report by President Kennedy's Advisory Committee on Labor-Management Policy, a group of top union and management officials plus some of the most experienced neutrals in labor relations:

> All members of this Committee are convinced that free collective bargaining should constitute the primary procedure by which the essential terms and conditions of employment shall be determined....
>
> When obstinate industrial disputes have occurred, involving strikes in important industries, there has been an inclination to question the efficacy of collective bargaining. Its record emerges, nevertheless, as one of outstanding progress within a single generation.
>
> ....
>
> We are opposed to any governmental imposition in peacetime of substantive terms and conditions on the parties.
>
> We reject the idea that there should be any legal requirement that disputes be resolved through compulsory arbitration.[3]

Sixteen months later, President Kennedy nevertheless proposed compulsory arbitration to settle a railroad dispute and Congress approved by an overwhelming vote.

Why does this conflict persist between expert opinion concerning large-scale strikes and the attitudes of the public (and many of its representatives)? One easy answer is that newspapers play up strike stories to build circulation and this so inflames their gullible readers that they forget strikes hardly hurt at all. Another easy answer is that the experts really know there is a strike problem, but labor and management couldn't

---

[3]*Collective Bargaining,* A Report by the President's Advisory Committee on Labor-Management Policy (Washington: GPO, 1962), p. 1.

Introduction

care less about the public interest and the professional neutrals would be unemployed if they offended either power bloc.

Unfortunately, the problems in this field refuse to yield to such easy answers. First, is the public really disenchanted with large-scale strikes, or do the politicians read too much into antilabor editorials and sporadic demands that somebody ought to pass a law? Do union members and lower-level managers share their leaders' opinions on strike controls? And just why do these leaders, and many independent experts, so vigorously oppose stringent controls over strikes? In short, we need to know just how serious the apparent disagreement is over this vital issue of public policy.

Second, and perhaps the most difficult of all questions in this area, just where is the dividing line between an emergency strike and other strikes? Nearly every strike obviously inconveniences some innocent bystanders, but it is not at all obvious how many inconveniences add up to an emergency justifying government intervention. Probably most disagreements over strike laws are, in fact, disagreements over whether emergency strikes are a rare or common occurrence. What do the facts show about the impact of past strikes? Have they really created any emergencies?

Third, regardless of whether strike controls are a good thing in principle, how have those now on the books worked in practice? The relevant provisions of the Taft-Hartley and Railway Labor Acts have been assailed for years by labor, management, and neutrals alike. Are these laws actually that bad? If so, why haven't they been changed?

Finally, if current strike controls are judged to be too harsh or too lenient, what other policy would be any better? This challenge to "put up or shut up" will effectively squelch some critics—but not many, for there are several alternative policies that might be adopted. Between the extremes of compulsory arbitration and a laissez-faire approach lie mediation, fact-finding, strike votes, injunctions, seizure, the "statutory strike," the choice-of-procedures technique, banning industry-wide bargaining, and applying the antitrust laws to unions. What are the advantages and disadvantages of these many alternatives?

These, then, are the principal questions to be explored in this book. *It should be noted that the emphasis will be on the emergency strike issue as it appears in peacetime and in private industry.* The distinction between peace and war is admittedly a fine one these days, but for our purposes it is sufficient to say that in an all-out conflict, such as World War II, nearly everyone accepts the need for strike controls and most of the above questions are considered purely academic. On the other hand, strikes by government employees, while certainly of practical interest today, present such unique legal and political problems that they deserve separate consideration.[4]

---

[4]See Kurt L. Hanslowe, *The Emerging Law of Labor Relations in Public Employment,* ILR Paperback No. 4, and Andrew W. J. Thomson, *Strikes and Strike Penalties in Public Employment,* Public Employee Relations Report 2, both published in 1967 by the New York State School of Industrial and Labor Relations at Cornell University, Ithaca, N.Y.

I

Is Anybody Listening?[1]

THE CASE FOR FREE COLLECTIVE
bargaining—and against strike controls—has been argued
eloquently and repeatedly over the years before congressional
committees, in union and management speeches and publi-
cations, and in a torrent of books and articles by independent
experts. Yet, whenever a major strike erupts, public opinion is
blamed for forcing the government intervention that nearly
always occurs. Is no one out there listening to those who are
experienced in labor relations?

The answer to that question is of considerable importance.
If public opinion is not as hostile to the strike as many government officials assume, then they might be less anxious to
intervene in labor disputes, a result devoutly hoped for by
many professionals. On the other hand, if there is a "communications gap" on this subject between the public and the professionals, who is leading and who is lagging? Does the layman
need more education on the advantages of free collective bargaining, or should the expert reexamine his attitudes toward
government intervention?

---

[1] I cheerfully acknowledge the piracy of this title from William H.
Whyte, Jr., *Is Anybody Listening? How and Why U.S. Business Fumbles
When It Talks with Human Beings* (New York: Simon and Schuster, 1952).

1

National Emergency Strikes

To determine whether anyone is listening, we shall examine what the experts have been saying about the strike and then what the public's attitudes are on this subject.

The Case for Free Collective Bargaining

In labor relations, as in other fields, expert opinion is seldom unanimous on any issue. Management and union officials certainly disagree with each other about many aspects of large-scale strikes, as we shall see in later chapters, and there is also division within the ranks of each of these groups. As for the neutrals, such as mediators, arbitrators, and scholars, total agreement on anything would be viewed by them as a near disaster. Add to all this the fact that there are no opinion polls for this specialized group, and it becomes evident that the phrase, "expert opinion," can be highly misleading in this context.

A review of the voluminous literature on emergency strikes will nevertheless reveal a surprising degree of consensus among union and management spokesmen and experienced neutrals. This consensus is primarily on general principles rather than specific policies, and even in principle such phrases as "the public interest," "good labor relations," or "industrial peace" can obviously mean different things to different people. With all of these caveats, however, it is still fair to say that most expert opinion in this country strongly favors free collective bargaining, meaning *"the opportunity for labor and management to work out their own problems and to arrive at voluntary agreement concerning them."*[2]

In terms of basic values, the case for free collective bargaining is essentially the same as the case for other political and economic liberties. In the political sphere, a free society recognizes the inevitability of conflicting views and interests, the danger of assuming that any individual or group has a mon-

[2]*Collective Bargaining*, A Report by the President's Advisory Committee on Labor-Management Policy (Washington: GPO, 1962), p. 1, italics added.

opoly on truth, and the consequent advantages in most circumstances of voluntary compromise over the government edict. In the marketplace, the essence of free enterprise is the belief that the public interest will best be served by the pursuit of self-interest and the clash of competing buyers and sellers. For all its faults, argue the supporters of collective bargaining, this institution measures up remarkably well to these tenets of a free society: in the world of work, it provides an orderly method for those directly involved to compromise their inevitable differences, both economic and noneconomic.

There is, of course, a place for the rule of law in this model of free collective bargaining, just as there is in our conceptions of freedom in speech or religion or enterprise. Liberty no more means anarchy in labor relations than in any other part of society. But the avowed purpose of our labor laws, such as the Wagner and Taft-Hartley Acts, has been not to supplant collective bargaining but to establish the ground rules necessary to make bargaining as effective and equitable as possible.

When stated in these general terms, the case for free collective bargaining is unassailable—but it also begs most of the hard questions in which we are interested. In the abstract, no one is ever against liberty or for compulsion. But what does all this have to do with the power of the strike to disrupt the lives of those not directly involved? Why not settle labor disputes, as we settle many other disputes, by an appeal to reason rather than brute force?

To these very practical questions, the advocates of private bargaining offer three equally practical answers: (1) the strike, or the threat of a strike, is necessary to make collective bargaining effective; (2) if left to run their natural course, few negotiations actually result in strikes and, of those stoppages that do occur, few if any seriously damage the public; and (3) the alternative of government intervention often creates more problems than it solves. Each of these claims deserves examination at this point, for together they constitute the core of the controversy over emergency strikes.

National Emergency Strikes

The Vital Function of the Strike[3]

In spite of the strike's long history and official sanction in the laws of the land, its precise role in collective bargaining remains widely misunderstood. Consider, for example, the frequent assertion that a particular strike, or even all strikes, would be unnecessary if the parties negotiated in good faith and based their decisions on reason rather than force. This counsel is about as helpful in labor disputes as it is in conflicts between buyers and sellers or Negroes and whites; most men do try to act reasonably and in good faith, but this standard of conduct inevitably means different things to different people.

For instance, assume a pair of negotiators who are genuinely men of good will and who are equally well versed in economics, labor law, statistics, and all other tools of the negotiator's trade. Is it so hard to believe that the union spokesman of this pair sincerely believes that his members deserve a 15-cent wage increase and some protection against losing their jobs to new machinery? Or that his management counterpart sincerely believes his company will be hurt competitively if it must give more than a 7-cent increase, or if it cannot introduce new machinery as rapidly as possible? Professional economists often disagree on such issues, and yet many observers are indignant when professional negotiators have the same trouble agreeing on what the future consequences will be of the many possible decisions they can make.

Most important, however, is the question, "In the event of disagreement, for whatever reason, what is to prevent management from winning every time?" This is putting the matter baldly, but accurately. If you don't like the Democrats, you can vote Republican; if you don't like the prices at one store, you can try another; but what do you do if your employer, with all the good will in the world, honestly disagrees with your

---

[3]This section is largely excerpted from my bulletin, *Negotiating Labor-Management Contracts* (Ithaca: New York State School of Industrial and Labor Relations, Cornell University, 1965) Bulletin 56, pp. 2–4.

Is Anybody Listening?

arguments for a 15-cent wage hike and more job security? You can, of course, quit and look for another job, but this is hardly what Congress meant, in such laws as the Wagner and Taft-Hartley Acts, when it said that workers could have an equal voice in such questions. In our example, as in real life, so long as the workers can only talk but not act, they obviously must continue to work on management's terms—their wages remain the same as before, and management remains free to introduce new machinery and to lay off workers as it sees fit.

And here lies the nub of the problem. If the mere right to talk is not enough, what kind of pressure should workers be able to put on a management which is otherwise able to win every argument? There seem to be but three alternatives: allow the workers only the right to quit and go elsewhere, a method which Congress felt to be unduly harsh and often ineffective; allow the workers to appeal to some government agency with the power to force the employer to do anything the government thinks right and good, a method opposed in principle by both political parties as well as by labor and management; or, third, allow workers to attempt to cut off their employers' income temporarily, by means of a strike. Thus, while the strike weapon can be crude and harmful, we know no better way of granting workers an *effective* voice in resolving the disagreements that inevitably arise between employer and employed.

For the same reasons, it is usually wrong to assume that the lockout is the employer's equivalent of the strike and, because unions strike far more often than employers lock out, unions must bear the blame for most work stoppages. Employers may sometimes find a lockout helpful, it is true, as when the Teamsters struck just some members of the multiemployer truckers' association in 1967, prompting the other employers to lock out their workers all across the country in order to preserve a solid front. In the vast majority of cases, however, management is ahead in the bargaining game as long as its employees continue to work.

In the above hypothetical example, for instance, after negotiations have stalled over union demands for 15 cents and restrictions on new machinery, what possible advantage could there be for management in locking out the workers? As we have seen, so long as the union only talks rather than acts, the workers continue to produce on the old wage scale, the company continues to introduce new machinery, and the pressure to fish or cut bait is entirely on the union. By a lockout, the company enormously increases the pressure on itself by cutting off its production and profits. Management's real power in a labor dispute is therefore its ability to confront a union with this difficult choice: either accept the employer's last offer so that the union's members may continue working and earning, or try to get more by a strike which will cut off the workers' own income as well as the company's.

The strike is thus defended as vital to effective bargaining, *even if it is seldom used.* The mere availability of this weapon reminds the parties that both may be hurt if they fail to settle their differences around the bargaining table. Without this "club in the closet," it is argued, negotiators would have little incentive to settle anything.

The Overrated Effects of the Strike

The strike may be useful to the private institution of collective bargaining, for the reasons just described, but what about its cost to the rest of society? In the postwar period, for example, we have averaged nearly four-thousand strikes a year in this country, which hardly suggests a seldom-used weapon, and many of these strikes have occurred in key industries. How do the experts explain away these hard facts?

We shall explore this issue more thoroughly in the next chapter, but the gist of the experts' case can be quickly given. First, they argue, it is illuminating to compare the number of strikes that *do* occur with the number of bargaining relationships in which strikes *might* occur. Although no one really knows how many labor-management contracts there are in the United States, estimates generally range between 75,000 and

Is Anybody Listening?

150,000.[4] Arbitrarily selecting the midpoint of this range (112,500) and dividing that into the annual average of strikes (4,000), we find that in an average year strikes probably occur in *fewer than 4 percent* of all bargaining relationships. Considering the many disagreements that can arise each year in even a single relationship, it is clear that the right to strike is actually exercised in only a microscopic portion of labor-management quarrels.

Further, in this small share of disputes that are not settled peacefully, there are few work stoppages large enough even to catch the public's eye, much less to create serious damage. In 1966, as a typical example, 50 percent of all strikes involved fewer than 100 workers and 72 percent involved fewer than 250 workers. As for the headline-catching strikes of over 10,000 workers, these totaled only 26 of the 4,405 stoppages that occurred in 1966.[5] In the face of these facts, it is asked, who can seriously argue that all strikes should be banned to protect the public?

By this reasoning, most experts reduce the emergency strike issue to one involving at most a handful of stoppages. And even among these large-scale strikes, they argue, few if any really have disastrous effects. On the one hand, a strike against a giant company such as General Motors or General Electric will certainly involve many thousands of workers but, unless the strike is industry-wide in scope, there will be competitors only too happy to continue supplying the public. As a matter of fact, autos and electrical manufacturing are two of the many industries that have never been completely shut down by a strike.

On the other hand, when an entire industry does go down, the strike's defenders warn against underestimating the resiliency of a modern economy. Many products, such as coal, can

---

[4]The lower estimate is from Bureau of National Affairs, *Collective Bargaining Negotiations and Contracts* (Washington, D.C., 1965), Binder Two, p. 32:22; the higher is from Elizabeth Jager, "Why Strikes?" *The American Federationist,* November 1965, p. 7.

[5]U.S. Bureau of Labor Statistics, "Work Stoppages in 1966," Summary Release, July 1967, Table 3.

be stockpiled before a strike begins; other goods and services have close substitutes to which consumers can turn, such as auto or air travel during a rail strike; in some cases, such as petroleum refining and the telephone industry, automation has progressed to such a point that supervisors alone can maintain operations during a strike; for a few products, such as steel and copper, foreign sources can sometimes be substituted for struck domestic sources; and many industries have excess capacity which can be used to make up temporary shortages after a strike has ended. In short, this argument goes, there are very few goods or services that the public cannot do without for a short period, and there are even fewer that are likely to be cut off completely by a strike.

But what if a major strike continued for a year or two, instead of the "short period" in which the public can presumably get along? On this point, too, the experts are virtually unanimous. Such a question, they say, ignores the essentially conservative nature of collective bargaining. No union wants to keep its members out of work indefinitely, and no employer wants to go bankrupt fighting a union. By cutting off the income of both parties, a strike generates enormous pressures upon them, or at least upon the weaker of the two in any particular relationship, and it soon becomes cheaper to settle than to continue the fight. It is therefore no accident that, in 1966, 43 percent of all strikes lasted less than a week, 79 percent less than a month, and 95 percent less than three months.[6] In fact, only twice in our history has an entire industry been shut down by a strike lasting longer than three months: in 1959, when basic steel was struck for 116 days, and in 1967–1968, when the copper industry was struck for 8½ months.[7]

---

[6]*ibid.*, Table 2.

[7]The rubber strike of 1967 shut down three of the five largest tire companies for three months, but the other two were only struck for three weeks or less. One bituminous coal strike began on September 19, 1949 and did not officially end until March 5, 1950, but during that period there were some individual settlements, a three-week truce, and several three-day work weeks. Chamberlain and Schilling's description of this as one 146-day

Is Anybody Listening?

It is facts such as these that lead many observers to conclude that few strikes, if any, have ever triggered a peacetime emergency in the past, or are likely to do so in the future.

The Hazards of Strike Controls

Not all experts are equally enthusiastic about every aspect of free collective bargaining. Many employers, for example, believe that excessive union power does create strike emergencies, and many unionists charge that the strength of particular employers can rob the right to strike of any bargaining effectiveness. On the third argument in favor of private bargaining, however, nearly all the professionals of every camp are in overwhelming agreement: there is no such thing as a good antistrike law, only a choice among several poor alternatives.

We shall investigate the various shades of this opinion in later chapters, when we discuss the criticisms made of current strike controls in the Taft-Hartley and Railway Labor Acts and the disagreement over how these laws could be improved. At this point, it will suffice to describe the experts' case against compulsory arbitration, for this is the most extreme alternative to private bargaining and therefore illustrates most sharply the perils of all types of strike control.

By compulsory arbitration, we mean a law stating that, in some or all union-management relationships, the strike is prohibited and unresolved disputes must instead be submitted to an impartial body whose decisions will be final and binding upon the parties. Although such a law would seem to promise industrial peace and the substitution of equity for the raw power of the strike, critics charge that its actual results would be very different.

First, they predict, such a law would actually *increase* the number of unresolved labor disputes. We have seen that, when

"partial" strike therefore seems accurate. Neil W. Chamberlain and Jane Metzger Schilling, *The Impact of Strikes* (New York: Harper and Brothers, 1954), p. 124.

the chips are down, relatively few union-management disagreements are put to the costly test of a strike. If the penalty for disagreement is not a strike, however, but a gentlemanly hearing before some government board, why should either party, and particularly the weaker one, give anything away in negotiations when he just might win it later in arbitration? And since both parties expect arbitrators to split the difference between opposing positions, each has another incentive to maintain an extreme position throughout negotiations. Thus, it is said, instead of compulsory arbitration being used only to settle the few disputes that now erupt into serious strikes, it would so undermine the bargaining process that deadlocks would becomes the rule instead of the exception, the arbitration machinery would be flooded with cases, and the government would end up having to resolve many trivial issues as well as most serious differences between the parties.

And once the parties are before some labor court, why is there an assumption that this court's decision will be any better than a decision reached as part of a strike settlement? Arbitrators no more know what a "fair wage" is than does anyone else, nor do they agree on what are management's rights and what are not, nor has the truth been revealed to them concerning the right-to-work question or any other contentious issue. In addition, a solution imposed by an outsider is often felt to be less satisfying to those involved than one they have worked out for themselves. This can be a particularly fatal defect in labor relations, where the winners and losers, unlike most litigants, must continue to work together after the court hands down its decision.

This weakness of compulsory arbitration in turn raises the ugly spector of enforceability. If a union finds an arbitration award repugnant, just how can the government stop an illegal strike by workers who, in an emergency situation, would probably number in the thousands? Send in the troops? When the coal miners were ignoring various government threats in the 1940's, their defiant cry was, "You can't dig coal with

bayonets!" and no one has yet thought of an effective rejoinder. Even during World War II, when organized labor's
no-strike pledge was coupled to patriotic fervor and the government's awesome emergency powers, there were nevertheless
over 16,000 strikes in the period of 1942 through 1945. In
recent years, the difficulty of enforcing strike bans has been
dramatically and repeatedly illustrated in the field of government employment, as nurses, teachers, subway workers, garbage
collectors, and other public workers have struck in defiance of
antistrike laws. Injunctions, seizure, fines, and jail sentences
have all been thrown against strikes at one time or another,
and none has a perfect record of compliance.

Finally, its critics charge that compulsory arbitration has
practical implications that extend far beyond labor relations.
Although management, for example, is certainly not enamored
of the strike, it has long feared that controls in the labor market
could soon lead to controls in the product market. How could
Congress declare that the price of labor, and therefore workers'
income, should be fixed "in the public interest," and yet leave
employers free to get as much as they can in all other price
and profit decisions? Thus, the end of free collective bargaining
might eventually spell the end of free enterprise.

Summary

This, then, is the impressive case that the experts mount for
free collective bargaining in general and the strike in particular: both are in harmony with the values of a democratic
society; the strike threat is necessary to induce voluntary
compromise at the bargaining table; the strikes that do occur
are vastly overrated as to their frequency and their impact
upon the public; and antistrike laws are a cruel hoax, unable
to produce either more peace or more justice in the labor
market. It should be reiterated that this is not the unanimous
view of every union leader, management official, and labor
scholar in the country, but it is the tenor of majority opinion

in this group. The next question is how well the experts have sold their case to the public at large.

The Public's Opinion of Strikes

One social scientist has said that modern public opinion polls "represent the most useful instrument of democracy ever devised."[8] Not many people are that enthusiastic about polls, for they abound in problems of construction and interpretation. Questions are raised, for example, about the adequacy of the pollsters' samples, the validity of reducing complex issues into a single question and a yes-no choice of answers, the difficulty of measuring the sincerity or intensity of responses, and many similar problems.

But if you want to know where this huge and diverse American public stands on an issue such as strikes, what other source can match even the questionable accuracy of opinion polls? Certainly not a few letters to the editor, nor the sidewalk interviews of a TV reporter, nor even the outcome of national elections, since these seldom turn on any single issue. We shall therefore use opinion polls for the same reason others use them, "not because of their excellence but because of the unavailability of anything superior."[9]

The 1935–1949 Period

Our task is simplified by the fact that Chamberlain and Schilling[10] have already analyzed the poll data on strikes gathered in the period from the mid-1930's, when the modern opinion poll was born, through 1949. We shall first summarize their findings and then compare them with the results of more recent polls.

First, the polls of that period indicated that public opinion

---

[8]Samuel Stouffer, as quoted by George Gallup in *Gallup Political Index* (American Institute of Public Opinion), Report no. 5, October 1965, p. 1.

[9]Neil W. Chamberlain, assisted by Jane Metzger Schilling, *Social Responsibility and Strikes* (New York: Harper and Brothers, 1953), p. 41.

[10]*ibid.*, chs. 3–5.

was decidedly more hostile to strikes than to any other aspect of union behavior, including featherbedding, demands for compulsory membership, and pressure for higher wages.

Second, as might be expected, "substantial majorities" favored rigorous control of strikes occurring during wartime and "in peacetime under emergency conditions, such as preparation for defense or reconversion from war to civilian production."[11]

Third, regarding strikes under "normal peacetime conditions," minorities of up to one third favored outlawing *all* such strikes, and up to two-thirds of those polled were for banning the strike in particular industries. For example, from 43 to 64 percent (depending on the industry and year) would have outlawed strikes in the electric, gas, telephone, local transportation, and railroad industries. Also, majorities consistently favored "almost any proposal" for postponing strikes without actually forbidding them, such as compulsory cooling-off periods, and these majorities increased "markedly" in size when the issue was narrowed to strikes in industries considered vital.[12]

Fourth, and perhaps most surprising, these researchers concluded that "the public's dissatisfaction with strikes...does not spring from a procompany or antiunion bias."[13] In several polls dealing with the merits of particular strikes in the postwar years, public sentiment tended either to be divided equally between the parties or to be more sympathetic to the strikers' position than to the management's. Moreover, when union members were singled out in a few polls, their view of strike controls proved to be only slightly less favorable than the general public's. In fact, on the basis of a 1946 poll that identified the views of "salaried executives" as well as those of union members, Elmo Roper reported, "despite the oft-stated rejection of compulsory arbitration by leaders of management

---

[11]*ibid.*, pp. 65–66.
[12]*ibid.*, pp. 70–73.
[13]*ibid.*, p. 75.

13

and labor, the idea has support from the rank and file of both."[14]

Thus, judging from these poll results, a majority of the American public clearly wanted strike controls of some kind during the peacetime as well as wartime years of 1935–1949. That period, however, was hardly an ideal time to argue the case for free collective bargaining. The country seemed to be in a perpetual state of emergency, as the Great Depression of the 1930's was followed by a world war, a postwar inflation, and the onset of the cold war with Russia. On the labor front itself, the public had never before witnessed collective bargaining throughout the basic industries and had never experienced as many strikes in a single year as it did in 1946. In retrospect, it is surprising that public opinion was not even more hostile to the strike in the pre-1950 period.

The Post-Korean Period

Of couse, the years from 1950 to 1968 have not been precisely idyllic. On the international scene, the period opened with the Korean War and closed with Vietnam, and the intervening years were punctuated by cold-war flare-ups in Berlin, Hungary, Cuba, and many other places. Since price and wage controls were in effect during the Korean War, those years are particularly ill-suited as a test of sentiment toward peacetime strikes, which are our primary concern, and are therefore omitted from this survey.

For better or for worse, however, the post-Korean years up to 1968 seem to have been about as "normal" as anyone can expect these days. On the home front, price and wage controls were lifted in 1953, the economy remained relatively stable and prosperous into the mid-1960's, strike activity trended downward during much of this period, collective bargaining was no longer a novelty, and during the "Eisenhower years" the national administration deplored excessive intervention in labor relations. It is doubtful that the case for free collective

---

[14]"The Fortune Survey," *Fortune*, vol. 34, no. 5 (November 1946), p. 16.

Is Anybody Listening?

bargaining will be heard under more favorable conditions than these in the near future.

Yet, the poll results shown in Table 1 indicate that the public continues to view the strike with a jaundiced eye.[15] Between one quarter and one half of those polled would outlaw some or all strikes even when, as in polls 1–4, they are offered no alternative method of settling disputes. When polls 5–8 offered such an alternative in the form of compulsory arbitration—the very antithesis of free collective bargaining —clear majorities rolled in on every suggested type of arbitration plan and from nearly every political quarter, occupational group, and geographic region. Finally, polls 9–11 suggest that, as in earlier years, the public is understandably more concerned over large-scale and "vital" strikes than others, and it is overwhelmingly in favor of controls that fall short of outright prohibition of the strike.

---

[15]The polls in Tables 1 and 2 were drawn primarily from three sources. From the Roper Public Opinion Research Center at Williams College, which collects and catalogues the output of several polling agencies, a list was obtained of all polls dealing with strikes that the Center had collected for the years 1954–1965. Of the total of 33 poll questions thus made available, 13 were selected as most relevant to this study. Also examined were several of the *Annual Labor Surveys* of the Opinion Research Corporation (Princeton, N.J.) and all issues of the *Gallup Political Index,* published by the American Institute of Public Opinion (Princeton, N.J.). Other sources used are indicated in the tables.

Table 1, p. 16 ff.

National Emergency Strikes

Table 1. Public Opinion on Strikes and Strike Controls, 1953–1967.

Outlaw the Strike?

Poll No. 1:
(February 1966)

"Would you favor or oppose a law which would make all strikes illegal?"

Favor:	27%
Oppose:	61
No opinion:	12

Poll No. 2:
(February 1960)

(a) "The right of labor unions to strike should be fully protected."

Agree:	52%
Disagree:	33
Don't know:	15

(b) "Strikes in large industries should be outlawed by the federal government."

Agree:	47%
Disagree:	39
Don't know:	14

Poll No. 3:
(December 1953 and January 1963)

"Do you think strikes by workers in communications industries—such as newspapers, telephone, radio, and TV—should or should not be forbidden by law?"

	1953	1963
Should:	38%	39%
Should not:	44	47
No opinion:	18	14

Poll No. 4:
(January 1963)

"Do you think strikes by workers in transportation industries—such as the railroads, airplanes, busses, and shipping—should or should not be forbidden by law?"

Should:	42%
Should not:	44
Don't know:	14

Adopt Compulsory Arbitration?

Poll No. 5:
(December 1959)

"A senator has made this proposal for settling labor disputes before nationwide strikes can start: if the unions and the companies can't reach an agreement, then a special court would hand down a decision which both sides would have to accept. Would you favor or oppose this proposal?"

	Total Sample	Union Members and Their Families
Favor:	59%	54%
Oppose:	21	30
No opinion:	20	16

Poll No. 6:
(January 1966)

"It has been suggested that no strike be permitted to go on for more than 7 days. If after 7 days the union and the employer cannot reach an agreement, a government-appointed committee would decide the issue and both would be compelled to accept the terms. Would you favor or oppose this idea?"

	Favor	Oppose	No Opinion
Total Sample:	58%	29%	13%
By occupation			
Professional & business:	49	39	12
White-collar:	55	29	16
Farmers:	66	21	13
Manual:	59	30	11
By political party			
Republican:	56	35	9
Democrat:	60	26	14
Independent:	57	30	13
By region			
East:	40	26	34
Midwest:	60	26	14
South:	56	32	12
West:	58	26	16

Poll No. 7:
(Spring 1967)

"It has been suggested that no strike be permitted to go on for more than 21 days. If after 21 days, the union and the employer cannot reach an agreement, the courts would appoint a committee that would decide the issue and both be compelled to accept the terms. Would you favor or oppose this idea?"

	Total Sample	Union Members and Their Families
Favor:	68%	55%
Oppose:	22	41
No opinion:	10	4

National Emergency Strikes

Poll No. 8:
(March 1963)

(a) "There have been a number of long strikes in different parts of the United States during the last year. Strikes sometimes are settled by arbitration in which a neutral person, or group of persons, decides on a settlement which both labor and management are bound to accept. Would you be in favor of, or against, having Congress pass a law that would require arbitration in any strike that lasted more than, say, 60 days?"

In favor:	82%
Against:	13
No opinion:	5

(b) "Some people say that getting the news is so important for the general public that no strikes should be permitted where newspapers, radio or television stations are involved. Instead, they say, there should be a requirement that disputes must be settled by arbitration in such cases. Do you agree with that view, or disagree?"

Agree:	55%
Disagree:	38
No opinion:	7

Adopt Other Controls?

Poll No. 9:
(February 1954)

"If you were in Congress, would you be for or against a law that says in industries considered vital to the country's welfare, the government may get a court order to prevent a strike for several months while settlements are being attempted?"

	Total Sample	Union Members
For:	87%	77%
Against:	8	20
No opinion:	5	3

Poll No. 10:
(January 1954)

"A federal law has been suggested, providing that before any labor union can call workers out on strike, there must be a secret vote of the workers, under government supervision, in which a majority say they are in favor of striking. Are you for or against such a law?"

For:	77%
Against:	14
No opinion:	9

18

Is Anybody Listening?

Poll No. 11:
(1956)

"If you were in Congress, would you be for or against a law to require unions to give 60 days' notice before they can go out on strike?"

	Total Sample	Union Members
For:	83%	71%
Against:	10	23
No opinion:	7	6

Sources: Poll No. 1: American Institute of Public Opinion (AIPO), *Gallup Political Index*, Report no. 9, p. 15. *No 2:* Texas Poll #1288 (as indexed by the Roper Public Opinion Research Center, Williams College, Williamstown, Mass.). *No 3:* AIPO #524 and #667 (Roper Center). *No. 4:* AIPO #667 (Roper Center). *No. 5:* George Gallup, "New Laws on Strikes Favored," *Los Angeles Times*, Dec. 4, 1959, p. 31. *No. 6:* AIPO, *Gallup Political Index*, Report no. 8, p. 11. *No. 7:* George Gallup, "New Plan to Curb Strikes Wins Public, Union Members' Approval," AIPO Release, April 26, 1967. *No. 8:* Minnesota Poll #222 (Roper Center). *No. 9:* Opinion Research Corporation, *1954 Labor Survey* (Princeton, N. J., 1954), p. A-20. *No. 10:* Minnesota Poll #123 (Roper Center). *No. 11:* Opinion Research Corporation, *Labor Unions in Politics* (Princeton, N. J., 1956), p. A-10.

Is this disenchantment with the strike a reflection of a deeper hostility toward collective bargaining in general and labor unions in particular? "No," said Chamberlain and Schilling for the pre-1950 period, and the same answer appears to hold true today.

It is easy, of course, to show impressive results to this effect with questions like, "In general, do you approve or disapprove of labor unions?" (72 percent approved in 1936 and 71 percent still approved in 1965);[16] or "On the whole, do you approve or disapprove of a law that guarantees workers the right to form unions and bargain with their employers?" (83 percent approved in 1944 and 76 percent in 1964).[17] Probably more meaningful than these generalized expressions of good will are the poll results presented in Table 2. In choosing sides in a

[16]American Institute of Public Opinion, *Gallup Political Index,* Report no. 5, October 1965, p. 14.

[17]Opinion Research Corporation (Princeton, N.J.): *1954 Labor Survey,* p. 15 and *Public Thinking on Labor Union Demands, 1964,* p. A-4.

specific strike, assessing blame for higher prices, and appraising employers' motives, the public today seems to be no more antiunion or promanagement than Chamberlain and Schilling found it to be in the 1930's and 1940's.

Needless to say, Table 2 is not meant to prove that the general public supports organized labor across the board. Other polls have shown public disapproval of featherbedding and compulsory union membership, and yet others have shown that more people think the laws regulating unions are "not strict enough" than think this of the laws regulating business.[18] The point nevertheless remains: the public's hostility to the strike cannot be dismissed as part of a general bias against all of labor's aims and methods. For further evidence of this, note the support of union members for strike controls in Table 1 (polls 5, 7, 9, and 11).

There are other interesting questions often raised in this area of public opinion and strikes, but most are of the "iffy" variety. For example, if polls were not influenced by current or recent strikes, what would they show? Poll number 5 in Table 1, for instance, was taken near the end of the 116-day steel strike of 1959, and that fact must surely have influenced the vote in favor of compulsory arbitration. But every year brings either the threat or the fact of a newsworthy strike, so how can one ever take an "uncontaminated" poll? Then if newspapers played down strike news, wouldn't that make public opinion more tolerant of stoppages? Probably, but no one will ever know the answer to that or similar questions.[19]

---

[18]Hazel Gaudet Erskine, "The Polls: Attitudes toward Organized Labor," *Public Opinion Quarterly*, vol. 26, no. 2 (Summer 1962), pp. 286–288. For some of the pitfalls of opinion polls, see those dealing with right-to-work laws. In a 1957 Gallup poll, for example, a plurality of 45% opposed such laws on one question (with 41% in favor and 14% undecided) and a majority of 73% then supported them when they were described differently in another question—both on the same poll. (*ibid.*, p. 286.)

[19]This study has not duplicated Chamberlain and Schilling's analysis of the intensity of public opinion concerning strikes, although this is a worthwhile area of investigation. Some of the poll questions they used

Is Anybody Listening?

Poll No. 1:
(August and December 1959)

"In the strike now going on between the steel workers union and the steel companies, are your sympathies with the union, or with the steel companies?"

	August	December
With union:	27%	27%
With companies:	32	28
Neither:	25	22
No opinion:	16	23

Poll No. 2:
(July 1956)

"From what you've heard or read, which side [in the current steel strike] do you think is more nearly in the right—the company, or the employees?"

Company:	34%
Employees:	27
No opinion:	39

Poll No. 3:
(June 1955)

"Which side [in the current strike at Ford Motor Company] are you on—the workers' or the company's?"

Workers':	37%
Company's:	18
Don't know or no answer	45

Poll No. 4:
(July 1959 and January 1961)

"Some people say that higher prices are caused largely by the demand for higher wages on the part of labor. Others say it's the demand for higher profits on the part of employers. Who do you think is more to blame—employees or employers?"

	1959	1961
Employees to blame:	33%	31%
Employers to blame:	37	26
Both or undecided:	30	43

for this purpose have not been repeated in recent years, and the available data are difficult to interpret. For example, in response to the question, "What do you think is the most important problem facing this country today?" strikes usually rank about fifth among the domestic problems cited, but they sometimes appear alone and sometimes are lumped under the heading of "labor problems, labor unions, strikes, etc." See AIPO #616, 618, 664, and 677 (as indexed by the Roper Center).

National Emergency Strikes

Poll No. 5: (1954 and 1964)   "Do you think most companies try to pay higher wages as they prosper, or do you think they have to be forced to pay higher wages?"

	1954	1964
Pay as they prosper:	38%	36%
Have to be forced:	52	52
Don't know:	10	12

Poll No. 6: (1954 and 1964)   "Do you think most companies would like to break the unions if they got a chance, or do you think they are willing to deal with the unions?"

	1954	1964
Like to break:	47%	46%
Willing to deal with:	40	38
Don't know:	13	16

Sources: Poll No. 1: George Gallup, "New Laws on Strikes Favored," *Los Angeles Times*, Dec. 4, 1959, p. 31. *No. 2:* American Institute of Public Opinion (AIPO) #567 (as indexed by the Roper Public Opinion Research Center). *No. 3:* AIPO #548 (Roper Center). *No. 4:* AIPO, as reported by Hazel Gaudet Erskine, "The Polls: Attitudes Toward Organized Labor," *Public Opinion Quarterly*, vol. 26, no. 2 (Summer 1962), p. 285. *Nos. 5* and *6:* Opinion Research Corporation (Princeton, N. J.), *1954 Labor Survey*, pp. A-2, 3, and *Public Thinking on Labor Union Demands*, 1964, pp. A-7, 8.

Conclusions

Is anybody listening to the experts who for years have been arguing the case for free collective bargaining? Apparently not. If there is one thing on which there is agreement among the leading members of the AFL-CIO, the National Association of Manufacturers, and the Industrial Relations Research Association, it is the belief that the right to strike (and to take a strike) is vastly superior to compulsory arbitration as a method for resolving union-management disagreements. Yet, not only does a majority of the "general public" persist in voicing approval for all types of strike controls, up to and including compulsory arbitration, but so do many (if not most) rank-and-file workers and managers. Roper noted this leader-member split as far back as 1946, and the poll results in Table 1 show that it has continued up to today.

Is Anybody Listening?

Opinion polls can, however, beguile the unwary reader into forgetting some obvious truths. For one thing, no one seriously claims that the majority is always right; for another, no one argues that leaders should never lead. Most important, there is a vast difference between the uncluttered world of the opinion poll, in which one can choose between black-and-white alternatives and bear no responsibility for results, and the real world of the policy maker. Only rarely, for example, does a President or Congressman face a clear choice between free collective bargaining and compulsory arbitration. The more likely choice will be between a little more or a little less intervention in murky disputes about which many people have strong opinions but few have any facts.

And you may be sure that one of the matters on which opinions will far outnumber the facts is whether a particular dispute is creating a public emergency. It is therefore time to move from the antiseptic world of theories and opinions to the complex world in which strikes actually occur. Do some of these work stoppages create emergencies or don't they?

II

Emergency Strikes: Fact or Fancy?

The strike is among the most highly publicized and the least studied social phenomena of our time.[1]

IN FEBRUARY OF 1968, NEW YORK City declared its first city-wide health emergency since 1931, in response to a nine-day strike by garbage collectors that had left uncollected nearly a hundred thousand tons of trash.[2] Across the Atlantic a short time before, quite a different strike had occurred when French police tried to prevent athletes from using drugs to pep up their performance. Outraged bike racers protested by dismounting as a body and walking all of one hundred yards in the middle of a twenty-two day race, "the first strike of professional athletes in defense of the needle"![3]

Most strikes obviously fall between these extremes of calamity and comedy—but just how far between is the great unanswered question in this field.

---

[1]Joel Seidman in the foreword to *Diary of a Strike*, by Bernard Karsh (Urbana: University of Illinois Press, 1958), p. v.

[2]*New York Times*, Feb. 9, 1968, p. 22 and Feb. 12, 1968, p. 42.

[3]*New York Times*, July 10, 1966, sec. 5, p. 5.

National Emergency Strikes

Consider, for example, the debate in this country over strikes in basic steel, an industry presumably crucial to the functioning of any modern economy. Near the end of a fifty-five day steel strike during the Korean War, the then Secretary of Defense said: "No enemy nation could have so crippled our production as has this work stoppage. No form of bombing could have taken out of production in one day 380 steel plants and kept them out nearly two months."[4] In fact, that was but one of five strikes that closed down the entire American steel industry for a total of 282 days, or over nine months, in the fourteen years from 1946 to 1959. Surely some or all of these stoppages were national emergencies? Both the Democratic and Republican administrations of those years thought so and tried to stop them with everything from Cabinet-level mediation to the injunction and seizure.

Then, following the 116-day strike of 1959, the U.S. Department of Labor launched a major study to determine "why the steel industry is continually plagued by strikes and what actions, if any, management and labor in the industry, or Government, can or should take to correct the situation."[5] To assure independence, the director of the project was appointed from outside the government, and he in turn drew upon the talents of many of the country's top specialists in labor relations. Based upon fourteen months of study, the project's final report stated flatly, "the public interest has not been seriously harmed by strikes in steel."[6] Further, since the effects of steel strikes on the public "are typically exaggerated" and in fact "need not cause alarm,"[7] it followed that the best government policy in future steel conflicts would be to intervene as little as possible:

---

[4]As quoted in Neil W. Chamberlain and Jane Metzger Schilling, *The Impact of Strikes* (New York: Harper and Brothers, 1954), p. 211.

[5]James P. Mitchell, Secretary of Labor, as quoted in U.S. Department of Labor, *Collective Bargaining in the Basic Steel Industry* (Washington: GPO, 1961), p. vii.

[6]*ibid.*, p. 18.

[7]*ibid.*, p. 17.

Emergency Strikes: Fact or Fancy?

> By far the most constructive alternative is the achievement by the parties [themselves] of a reduction in conflict. A minimum of Government intervention will assist the parties in achieving this goal. *Even if conflict is not substantially reduced, its consequences are of primary concern only to the parties.* The public interest...can easily be exaggerated.[8]

Do emergency strikes thus exist only in the overheated imagination of the public? Clearly we need some answer to this question before we can decide what government policy should be toward strikes. If there really are no emergency stoppages, let us scrap all controls and let the private parties go about their business. Or if only a few strikes create emergencies, let us make sure the government intervenes only in those and not in any others.

The only difficulty with this logical approach is that it requires both a yardstick to measure the effects of strikes and some agreement on where the "emergency line" is on that yardstick. Unfortunately, for reasons we shall now explore, we have neither the yardstick nor any agreement on how to read one if we had it.

The Aggregate Impact of Strikes

Forty-five years ago, a critic of unions devoted an entire book to the thesis that "non-production due to strikes was the basic cause of high prices" after World War I.[9] Today, few economists would claim that it is possible to isolate the total impact of strikes on prices or anything else, and most of the debate over strike effects now centers on whether particular work stoppages have created emergencies. In view of many people's misgivings about all strikes, however, a brief look at the aggregate record is in order.

Table 3 presents the government statistics frequently cited by the defenders of free collective bargaining. Whether viewed

---

[8]*ibid.*, pp. 3–4, italics added.

[9]Marshall Olds, *The High Cost of Strikes* (New York: G.P. Putnam's Sons, 1921), p. xvi.

Table 3. Strikes in the United States, 1927–1966.*

Year	Strikes Number	Strikes Average duration (calendar days)‡	Workers directly involved† Number (thousands)	Workers directly involved† Percent of total employed§	Man-days idle during year Number (thousands)||	Man-days idle during year Percent of estimated total working time¶	Union membership Number (thousands)**	Union membership Workers involved in disputes as percent of union members
1927	707	26.5	330	1.4	26,200	0.37	—	—
1928	604	27.6	314	1.3	12,600	.17	—	—
1929	921	22.6	289	1.2	5,350	.07	—	—
1930	637	22.3	183	.8	3,320	.05	3,162	5.8
1931	810	18.8	342	1.6	6,890	.11	3,142	10.9
1932	841	19.6	324	1.8	10,500	.23	2,968	10.9
1933	1,695	16.9	1,170	6.3	16,900	.36	2,805	41.7
1934	1,856	19.5	1,470	7.2	19,600	.38	3,448	42.6
1935	2,014	23.8	1,120	5.2	15,500	.29	3,609	31.0
1936	2,172	23.3	789	3.1	13,900	.21	3,932	20.1
1937	4,740	20.3	1,860	7.2	28,400	.43	5,563	33.4
1938	2,772	23.6	688	2.8	9,150	.15	5,850	11.8

Year								
1939	2,613	23.4	1,170	4.7	17,800	.28	6,339	18.5
1940	2,508	20.9	577	2.3	6,700	.10	7,055	8.2
1941	4,288	18.3	2,360	8.4	23,000	.32	8,410	28.1
1942	2,968	11.7	840	2.8	4,180	.05	9,818	8.6
1943	3,752	5.0	1,980	6.9	13,500	.15	11,383	17.4
1944	4,956	5.6	2,120	7.0	8,720	.09	12,153	17.4
1945	4,750	9.9	3,470	12.2	38,000	.47	12,088	28.7
1946	4,985	24.2	4,600	14.5	116,000	1.43	12,684	36.3
1947	3,693	25.6	2,170	6.5	34,600	.41	13,968	15.5
1948	3,419	21.8	1,960	5.5	34,100	.37	14,339	13.7
1949	3,606	22.5	3,030	9.0	50,500	.59	13,977	21.7
1950	4,843	19.2	2,410	6.9	38,800	.44	14,090	17.1
1951	4,737	17.4	2,220	5.5	22,900	.23	14,968	14.8
1952	5,117	19.6	3,540	8.8	59,100	.57	15,452	22.9
1953	5,091	20.3	2,400	5.6	28,300	.26	16,404	14.6
1954	3,468	22.5	1,530	3.7	22,600	.21	15,679	9.8
1955	4,320	18.5	2,650	6.2	28,200	.26	16,043	16.5
1956	3,825	18.9	1,900	4.3	33,100	.29	16,396	11.6
1957	3,673	19.2	1,390	3.1	16,500	.14	16,625	8.4
1958	3,694	19.7	2,060	4.8	23,900	.22	15,650	13.2

Table 3. Strikes in the United States, 1927–1966. (Continued)

Year	Strikes		Workers directly involved†		Man-days idle during year		Union membership	
	Number	Average duration (calendar days)‡	Number (thousands)	Percent of total employed§	Number (thousands)‖	Percent of estimated total working time¶	Number (thousands)**	Workers involved in disputes as percent of union members
1959..........	3,708	24.6	1,880	4.3	69,000	.61	15,449	12.2
1960..........	3,333	23.4	1,320	3.0	19,100	.17	15,539	8.5
1961..........	3,367	23.7	1,450	3.2	16,300	.14	15,118	9.6
1962..........	3,614	24.6	1,230	2.7	18,600	.16	14,884	8.3
1963..........	3,362	23.0	941	2.0	16,100	.13	—	—
1964..........	3,655	22.9	1,640	3.4	22,900	.18	—	—
1965..........	3,963	25.0	1,550	3.1	23,300	.18	—	—
1966..........	4,405	22.2	1,960	3.7	25,400	.19	—	—

Sources: Strike data from U.S. Bureau of Labor Statistics, "Work Stoppages in 1966," Summary Release, July 1967 and Techniques of Preparing Major BLS Statistical Series (Washington: GPO, 1955), Bulletin 1168, ch. 12. Union membership data from Leo Troy, Trade Union Membership, 1897–1962 (New York: National Bureau of Economic Research, 1965), Table 1, p. 1.

Notes to Table 3:

*The number of strikes and workers relate to those beginning in the year; average duration, to those ending in the year. Man-days of idleness include all stoppages in effect.

†Workers are counted more than once if they were involved in more than one stoppage during the year. The number of workers involved in a strike is the maximum number actually made idle in the establishment directly involved. No distinction is made between the actual participants in a strike and those respecting, or kept idle by, picket lines or those sent home by the employer when a stoppage in one department closes the entire plant.

‡Figures are simple averages; each stoppage is given equal weight regardless of its size.

§"Total employed" refers to all workers employed in private industry. Employment in agriculture and government is not included because, until recently, there was little union organization and few strikes in those sectors of the labor force. Before 1951, a few other groups were also excluded, such as executives in private industry, but the data are generally comparable over time.

‖Man-days of idleness are based on the idleness at the establishments directly involved. Workers involved multiplied by days of idleness equal total man-days idle. Holidays and days not normally worked are omitted from this calculation.

¶"Estimated total working time" is computed by multiplying the average number of employed workers [see § above] by the number of days worked by most employees. This number excludes Saturdays when customarily not worked, Sundays, and established holidays.

**Total membership of American unions, exclusive of Canadian members. Comparable data not available for 1927–1929 or for the years since 1962.

over time or for any given year, these figures bear impressive witness to the relative insignificance of strikes in the economy as a whole. Although union membership has quadrupled in size since the mid-1930's, the number of stoppages per year has no more than doubled over the same period; in fact, strike activity declined sharply from the 1946–1955 decade (an average of 4,328 strikes per year) to the 1956–1965 decade (3,619 per year). In this most recent decade, too, fewer than one in twenty employees in private industry—and probably fewer than one of every eight or nine union members—have struck in any year, and the average strike has lasted only three weeks.

Note particularly the data on man-days of idleness directly resulting from strikes. In the forty-year period for which figures are available, strike idleness has rarely equalled 0.5 percent of total working time in private industry, and it has exceeded 1.0 percent only in the year 1946. In contrast, the Secretary of Labor noted in 1962 that *"more man-hours of production have been lost in the last 11 months because of unemployment than in the last 35 years because of strikes."*[10] Also in the same year, when strike losses totaled 18,600,000 man-days, on-the-job injuries and accidents cost the economy 39 million lost man-days.[11]

Critics of the strike, on the other hand, argue that gross totals and simple averages can be as misleading in this field as in any other. Table 4 shows that, in the typical peacetime year, one quarter to one half or more of all strike idleness has been concentrated in a handful of large-scale disputes. More specifically, Table 5 indicates that 78 percent of all work stoppages in 1964 involved only a single establishment—but the 1 percent involving fifty or more establishments rolled up 36 percent of all the man-days lost in that year's strikes.

In short, while these aggregate data should dispel some of the

[10]W. Willard Wirtz, as quoted in the *New York Times,* Nov. 26, 1962, p. 15, italics added.

[11]Fred W. Schmidt, Jr., "Preliminary Estimates of Work Injuries in 1962," *Monthly Labor Review,* vol. 86, no. 4 (April 1963), pp. 418–420.

Emergency Strikes: Fact or Fancy?

Table 4. Strikes Involving 10,000 Workers or More, Selected Periods.*

Period	Number	Workers directly involved		Man-days idle	
		Number (*thousands*)	Percent of total for period	Number (*thousands*)	Percent of total for period
1935–39 (average).........	11	365	32.4	5,290	31.2
1945.............	42	1,350	38.9	19,300	50.7
1946.............	31	2,920	63.6	66,400	57.2
1947.............	15	1,030	47.5	17,700	51.2
1948.............	20	870	44.5	18,900	55.3
1949.............	18	1,920	63.2	34,900	69.0
1950.............	22	738	30.7	21,700	56.0
1951.............	19	457	20.6	5,680	24.8
1952.............	35	1,690	47.8	36,900	62.6
1953.............	28	650	27.1	7,270	25.7
1954.............	18	437	28.5	7,520	33.3
1955.............	26	1,210	45.6	12,300	43.4
1956.............	12	758	39.9	19,600	59.1
1957.............	13	283	20.4	3,050	18.5
1958.............	21	823	40.0	10,600	44.2
1959.............	20	845	45.0	50,800	73.7
1960.............	17	384	29.2	7,140	37.4
1961.............	14	601	41.4	4,950	30.4
1962.............	16	318	25.8	4,800	25.8
1963.............	7	102	10.8	3,540	22.0
1964.............	18	607	37.0	7,990	34.8
1965.............	21	387	25.0	6,070	26.0
1966.............	26	600	30.6	7,290	28.7

Sources: U.S. Bureau of Labor Statistics, *Analysis of Work Stoppages, 1965* (Washington: GPO, 1966), Bulletin 1525, Table 2, and U.S. BLS, "Work Stoppages in 1966," Summary Release, July 1967, Table 3.

*For a description of the strike measures used, see Table 3.

wilder notions about strike activity, they do not really come to grips with the emergency issue. The figures on man-days of idleness, for instance, refer only to the time lost by the workers "directly involved" in a strike; they contain no clue to the un-

Table 5. Strikes by Number of Establishments Involved, 1964.

Number of establishments involved*	Strikes beginning in 1964		Workers directly involved		Man-days idle, 1964 (all strikes)	
	Number	Percent	Number	Percent	Number	Percent
Total..........................	3,655	100.0	1,640,000	100.0	22,900,000	100.0
1 establishment.................	2,843	77.8	582,000	35.5	6,620,000	28.9
2 to 5 establishments...........	419	11.5	196,000	12.0	2,840,000	12.4
6 to 10 establishments..........	133	3.6	130,000	7.9	1,890,000	8.3
11 establishments or more.......	155	4.2	585,000	35.7	9,790,000	42.7
11 to 49 establishments.........	114	3.1	119,000	7.3	1,550,000	6.8
50 to 99 establishments.........	12	.3	295,000	18.0	6,490,000	28.3
100 establishments or more......	23	.6	168,000	10.2	1,670,000	7.3
Exact number not known†.........	6	.2	2,760	.2	72,400	.3
Not reported....................	105	2.9	147,000	9.0	1,790,000	7.8

Source: U.S. Bureau of Labor Statistics, Analysis of Work Stoppages, 1964 (Washington: GPO, 1965), Bulletin 1460, Table 12, p. 20. Because of rounding, sums of individual items may not equal totals.

*An establishment is defined as a single physical location where business is conducted, or where services or industrial operations are performed; for example, a factory, mill, store, mine, or farm. A stoppage may involve one or two establishments or more of a single employer, or it may involve different employers.

†Information available indicates more than 11 establishments involved in each of these stoppages.

34

employment a strike may indirectly cause in other plants or industries. Or the same figures might well overstate the impact of strikes, for they allow no offset for the extra hours often worked before or after a stoppage. Finally, in none of these tables does the figure of the consumer ever appear. What happens to him when a particular plant or industry goes down in a labor dispute?

The Impact of Specific Strikes

For all the reasons above, it has long been clear that aggregate strike data are never going to settle the question of whether particular strikes do or do not create emergencies. Yet, there have been surprisingly few studies of the impact of specific strikes in the past on which we can draw for policy guidance in the future. The few studies available are nevertheless provocative and demand review at this point.

Case Studies

It should be stressed at the outset that the following summaries cannot do full justice to the studies under review. Our aim is only to indicate the "yardstick" each author used to measure strike effects, and to summarize his major conclusions.

The Warren study[12] reviewed the *New York Times* and the *Los Angeles Times* for the years 1914–1949 and found that 165 labor disputes made the front pages of both papers during those years and could thus be classed as the subject of country-wide public concern. The author then compared the news accounts of these disputes with this definition of a national emergency strike: "one which has resulted in a dangerous curtailment of supplies of necessary goods or services where substitutes are not available."[13] His conclusion:

[12]Edgar L. Warren, "Thirty-Six Years of 'National Emergency' Strikes," *Industrial and Labor Relations Review,* vol. 5, no. 1 (October 1961), pp. 3–15.

[13]*ibid.,* p. 13.

National Emergency Strikes

From this definition it may be seen that few strike situations can result in national emergencies during peacetime. Forty percent of those strikes which have attracted nationwide attention...were in industries where "necessary goods and services" were not involved [such as automobiles]. Another 24 percent did not result in a "dangerous curtailment of supplies" because they were in industries where the product could be stock-piled and stock piles were never entirely exhausted [such as coal mining]. Of strikes in those industries producing necessary goods and services, where a dangerous curtailment of supplies might have been created [such as shipping], there were no more than twenty of extended duration; and it may be assumed that in most of these situations the strikes were not entirely successful and substitute facilities were available. Only in the field of public utilities and transportation do we find instances of strikes which come within the definition of national emergencies, and even these industries produce few real crises.[14]

The first Christenson study[15] focused on bituminous coal mining, which was "responsible for a larger volume of dispute time losses than any other single industry"[16] in the 1930–1950 period. By a monthly comparison of coal output and man-days lost in coal strikes from 1933 to 1950, the author demonstrated that much of the output presumably lost during the coal strikes of those years was offset by increased output shortly before or after each strike, and in some cases by increased output during a strike from mines not directly involved. In fact, as strike idleness rose to all-time record levels after 1942, so did the output of coal; so great was the output volume that it is extremely doubtful whether, taking the [1942–1950] period as a whole, it would have been enhanced at all had there been no [labor] dispute time losses whatever."[17] This ability to offset strike losses so quickly was traced primarily to the enormous capacity of the coal industry, augmented during the 1940's by

---

[14]*ibid.*, pp. 14–15.

[15]C. Lawrence Christenson, "The Theory of the Offset Factor: The Impact of Labor Disputes upon Coal Production," *American Economic Review*, vol. 43, no. 4 (September 1953), pp. 513–547.

[16]*ibid.*, p. 513.

[17]*ibid.*, p. 547.

improved technology underground and the rapid development of strip mining aboveground.

In the second Christenson study,[18] the same author examined data on coal consumption over the 1934–1953 period and concluded that bituminous strikes had little effect on the consumption patterns of most coal users in those years. The one possible exception was the impact of some coal strikes on steel output, but this impact was judged to be temporary and of no effect on total steel output over the entire period.

The Bernstein and Lovell study[19] undertook an even more extensive analysis of the ten coal strikes that occurred in the years 1937–1950, a period during which "the miners spent approximately one year of the fourteen on strike."[20] In addition to examining the data on coal output itself, the authors also studied output trends in the industries which were then coal's major customers (steel, electric power, and railroads), general economic indicators (the indexes of industrial production and department store sales), and reports in the *New York Times* of other effects of the ten strikes on producers (such as layoffs in affected plants) and on consumers (such as the "brownouts" ordered in some cities and the rationing orders, school closings, and cutbacks in freight and passenger rail service). They then compared these findings with their three economic tests of a national emergency strike, "first, the strike must have an actual as distinguished from a potential effect; second, it must impose hardship rather than inconvenience; and, finally, its impact must be national rather than local."[21] Their conclusion:

---

[18]C. Lawrence Christenson, "The Impact of Labor Disputes upon Coal Consumption," *American Economic Review*, vol. 45, no. 1 (March 1955), pp. 79–112.

[19]Irving Bernstein and Hugh G. Lovell, "Are Coal Strikes National Emergencies?" *Industrial and Labor Relations Review*, vol. 6, no. 3 (April 1953), pp. 352–367.

[20]*ibid.*, p. 354.

[21]*ibid.*, p. 353.

National Emergency Strikes

None of the ten strikes studied created a national emergency. In fact, seven...had no serious effect at all. Only the two 1946 strikes and the stoppage of 1949–1950 reached the threshold of emergency. Each imposed inconveniences upon millions and hardship on a few in some communities and industries. Settlements came before these sporadic hardships could cumulate into a national crisis.[22]

In explaining why these strikes did not create emergencies, the authors emphasized, as did Christenson, the industry's excess capacity and the ability of users to stockpile coal before strikes began. Also, they stressed the economic and political pressures inducing labor and management to settle before a crisis was actually reached.

In the Bernstein study,[23] one of the above authors applied the same technique of analysis, and the same tests of an emergency impact, to the industry-wide strikes that occurred in steel and railroads in the 1946–1952 period. He concluded that the only nationwide rail stoppage of those years, a two-day strike in 1946, did meet his definition of a national emergency strike, in spite of its brief duration. "The railroad industry differs from both coal and steel in providing a service which cannot be stored. Hence the public impact of a rail strike is virtually immediate,"[24] and in 1946 this instant impact resulted in widespread layoffs, mail embargoes, the disruption of food deliveries and ocean shipping and long-distance and commuter passenger traffic, and traffic jams in large cities. "These reports, which could be multiplied several times over, leave no doubt that the 1946 rail strike was a national emergency. One can only wonder what might have happened if it had continued for another three or four days."[25]

---

[22]*ibid.*, p. 365.

[23]Irving Bernstein, "The Economic Impact of Strikes in Key Industries" in *Emergency Disputes and National Policy*, Irving Bernstein, Harold L. Enarson, and R. W. Fleming, eds. (New York: Harper and Brothers, 1955), ch. 2, pp. 24–45.

[24]*ibid.*, p. 42.

[25]*ibid.*, p. 44.

Emergency Strikes: Fact or Fancy?

Of the three steel shutdowns in this period, Bernstein also classed one, the 55-day stoppage in 1952, as a national emergency. Although his decision rested partly on this strike's impact on the defense program during the Korean War, it appears that the other effects of this stoppage would alone have met his tests of an emergency. Thus, he stressed that this steel strike had a sharper impact than the other two on the output of industrial suppliers (such as coal and railroads) and customers (particularly autos), on the general economic indicators (such as department store sales), and on employment in other industries (estimating that "somewhere between 750,000 and 1,000,000 persons suffered some loss of working time").[26] "In view of the widespread hardship effects upon suppliers, consumers, employment, and the defense program, it seems appropriate to class the 1952 steel strike as a national emergency."[27] Bernstein's general conclusions from his two studies were as follows:

> Only three of fifty-one highly unionized industries in the United States have a national emergency potential: coal, steel, and railroads. In the nine years following World War II there was a total of eight nationwide strikes in these industries—four in coal, three in steel, one in railways. By applying the criteria of a national emergency (national impact, actual effects, and a showing of widespread hardship), two of the eight...were emergencies, four... were serious but failed to satisfy the criteria, and two...caused little public inconvenience. The results leave little doubt that the national emergency problem, in so far as it is economic in character, has been much exaggerated.[28]

The Livernash Study[29] was briefly described in the first pages of this chapter. Commissioned by the U.S. Department of Labor, this study explored several aspects of collective bargaining in basic steel, including the impact of the five major strikes

[26]*ibid.*, p. 41.

[27]*ibid.*, p. 42.

[28]*ibid.*, p. 44.

[29]U.S. Department of Labor, *Collective Bargaining in the Basic Steel Industry*. Professor E. Robert Livernash of Harvard University was the director of this study.

in this industry in the postwar period: 1946 (26 days), 1949 (45 days), 1952 (55 days), 1956 (36 days), and 1959 (116 days). First, the study tackled the question of whether the steel production lost during these strikes was lost to the economy permanently or just temporarily, and it found that in this industry as in coal, added output just before and after strikes frequently offset strike losses. For example:

> Under recession influences in 1958 . . . , production declined and the industry operated at about 61 percent of capacity, as the average for the year. But, during the first 6 months of 1959, the period just prior to the strike, production as a percent of capacity averaged 87.8. Following the settlement [in January 1960], production jumped within 2 months to about 96 percent of capacity, and continued at high levels until the inventory situation was balanced. *But it is significant that within 4 months after the strike, production began to decline.* By July 1960, production as a percent of capacity was much lower than the 1958 average.[30]

Second, to test the effect of these strikes on industries dependent upon steel for their raw materials, the study appraised trends in three sets of statistics: quarterly constant-dollar expenditures on the total durable goods component of the gross national product; quarterly constant-dollar sales of consumers' durables and producers' equipment; and changes in durable goods inventories. The study's general conclusion, as noted earlier, was that "the public interest has not been seriously harmed by strikes in steel."[31]

> . . . most strikes can last much longer (even in an industry as basic as steel) than is generally believed before the economy will be seriously hurt. History in steel indicates that once strikes really begin to be seriously felt over wide segments of the economy, presssure from those affected will in most instances bring about a settlement.[32]

---

[30]*ibid.*, p. 37, italics added.

[31]*ibid.*, p. 18.

[32]*ibid.*, p. 49.

Emergency Strikes: Fact or Fancy?

The Kennedy study[33] briefly surveyed the effects of some of the postwar stoppages in public utilities. Kennedy found, for instance, that a 25-day strike in 1947 against the New Jersey telephone system had the following impact: "dial service was relatively unaffected; emergency calls were completed; in communities where dial service was not furnished the service was approximately 20 percent of normal; interstate service was curtailed to about 40 percent of normal."[34] In four strikes by electrical power workers in various cities in 1945–1946, one for as long as 27 days, "essential services to residential, hospital, and government users were maintained"[35] by supervisors, and the same was true of two strikes (of two and eight days) in the gas industry in New Jersey. Although "serious economic losses"[36] resulted from the gas and electric power strikes, because of their impact on industrial users, Kennedy clearly felt that none of the utility strikes he examined was an emergency, for none resulted in "immediate jeopardy to public health and safety."[37]

The Barrington study[38] of the 1966 transit strike in New York City—a 13-day stoppage of all subway service and over 90 percent of bus service, both public and privately owned—is by far the most precise and objective of the impact studies.

---

[33]Thomas Kennedy, "The Handling of Emergency Disputes," *Proceedings of Second Annual Meeting, Industrial Relations Research Association* (IRRA, 1950), pp. 14–27. For a review of some of the same strikes examined by Kennedy, see Robert R. France and Richard A. Lester, *Compulsory Arbitration of Utility Disputes in New Jersey and Pennsylvania* (Princeton, N.J.: Industrial Relations Section, Princeton University, 1951).

[34]Brief on Behalf of Defendant, New Jersey Bell Telephone Co., in re: The State of New Jersey v. Traffic Telephone Workers' Federation of New Jersey, et al. in Chancery of New Jersey 158/37, p. 6, as quoted in Kennedy, p. 17.

[35]Kennedy, p. 18.

[36]*ibid.*, p. 19.

[37]*ibid.*, p. 26.

[38]New York City Transit Authority, *The Effect of the 1966 Transit Strike on the Travel Behavior of Regular Transit Users,* Prepared from a Survey Made by Barrington and Co. (New York City, 1967).

National Emergency Strikes

Within a month of the strike's termination, a research firm had begun a survey of its effects, based upon a systematic random sample of households throughout the metropolitan area and consisting of telephone interviews with 8,700 regular transit users and personal interviews with 1,700 other transit users in low income areas who were not telephone subscribers. Interview results were processed through a computer and presented in a detailed report which showed, among other findings, the following:

> Forty percent of workers normally using the subway or bus to go to work lost one or more work days during the strike. Fifteen percent did not get to work at all. Among low income workers (under $3,000 per year) the corresponding figures were 60% losing some time and 30% not working at all.
>
> This represents a total loss of at least 6 million man-days of work. No estimate can be made of the time lost by workers who worked less than their regular hours during the strike.
>
> The median length of the trip to work doubled for those who managed to get there, from about half an hour to one hour and six minutes....
>
> Shopping by users of the transit system was reduced by about 50% during the strike....
>
> Among users of the transit system for social, educational, recreational, and other personal activities, three-quarters put off some or all such activities.[39]

The authors offered no opinion as to whether these strike effects added up to an emergency.

A Trial Yardstick

Finally, the Chamberlain and Schilling study[40] merits particular attention, for it is easily the most ambitious attempt yet made to measure strike effects. Instead of trying to define the line between emergency strikes and all others, these authors began by constructing a rating scale to measure the effects of any strike, large or small. For each stoppage, this scale yields a single score or rating, the aim being to provide a uniform

[39]*ibid.*, p. iii.
[40]*The Impact of Strikes.*

42

standard for judging the relative impacts of different strikes.

Chamberlain and Schilling did not, however, single out any particular figure on their yardstick as the dividing line between emergency and non-emergency strikes:

> How serious a strike must become before the government is warranted in intervening is not a question that can be answered solely by statistics—it depends on the public's willingness to pay the price of a strike....
>
> But if the public is unwilling to pay the price of some strikes, then some means of measuring their cost—of more precisely ascertaining the price of strikes—must be discovered. Otherwise we shall be unable to distinguish between those strikes which the public accepts as "reasonably" priced and those whose cost must price them out of our culture.[41]

Thus, the rating scale was offered only as a tool by which the executive arm of the government might better measure the impact of various strikes and in turn make better policy decisions about those strikes. To expect such a tool actually to make strike policy, by telling the government when intervention is or is not warranted, is as unrealistic as expecting a price or production index to tell the government at which point it can act.

In constructing their scale, the authors first identified the following as the groups or "publics" that might be affected by any strike:

> (1) *household consumers* of the struck product; (2) the *"direct" producers,* by which is meant (a)...[nonstriking] members of the struck unit, (b) commercial users of the struck product, and (c) suppliers of the struck unit and its members; (3) the *"indirect" producers,* who are (a) the suppliers of the commercial users of the struck product and suppliers of the suppliers of the struck firm and (b) commercial users of the products of the commercial users of the struck product; and (4)...["*indirect*"] *household consumers* patronizing any of the "indirect" producers.[42]

Several subscales were then devised to measure how *necessary* a struck good or service is to each of these consumer and pro-

---

[41]*ibid.,* p. 252.

[42]*ibid.,* p. 12, italics added.

ducer groups, the extent to which their needs can be met by available *stocks,* and the acceptability of *substitutes* for the struck good or service. Each of these subscales was graduated from 0 to 10 (rather than just "emergency" or "non-emergency") and each, of course, could yield a different score for different groups and on different days during the same strike. These "urgency ratings" were then to be multiplied by the number of people in each of the groups affected by a strike, and the final result would be a "total strike rating" for a particular day of a particular strike.

Even this cursory description suggests the staggering number of theoretical and practical problems involved in constructing such a strike index. In a General Motors strike, for example, how do you estimate on a 0–10 scale the necessity of Chevrolets to consumers or the acceptability of Fords and Plymouths as substitutes? Also, where do you find the data necessary to trace the impact of such a strike through the layers of thousands of GM suppliers, the suppliers of *those* suppliers, other customers of these suppliers, and so on and on? And even if you could eventually solve these problems through long and intensive research, how would you solve them for a president or governor in the middle of an actual strike, when the "impact score" is changing day by day?

But since many people are in effect already offering answers to these impossible questions, every time they advise the government to go in or stay out of a strike, Chamberlain and Schilling believed it would be an improvement at least to systematize these guesses and hunches. They therefore tested their scale on seventeen steel, coal, and railroad strikes of the 1939–1952 period, using whatever data they could find and filling in the many gaps by assumption and inference. One of their most provocative findings was that producer effects (loss of income) outweighed consumer effects in all but one of these stoppages.

A strike may be serious not because it withholds final products from consumers but because it deprives employees in related industries of employment income. In recent years there has been a tendency to judge the impact of a strike in terms of the hardship it inflicts on ultimate consumers....If this view were followed consistently, however, it might permit a general strike throughout the automobile industry to be continued for months without government intervention, while a stoppage at a local utility would not be allowed to finish out a day.[43]

Such an approach, these authors argued, "overlooks the fact that loss of income can be as serious to some individuals as loss of goods is to others."[44]

An Appraisal

These case studies have made two vital contributions to the debate over strike controls. First, they have clearly demonstrated that the economic effects of a work stoppage are often less drastic than the casual observer is likely to assume. There *are* many ways in which the output apparently lost during a strike can be offset or recaptured, and there *are* many ways in which consumers can adapt to temporary shortages. The coal industry, for example, was shut down by strikes for a total of one year out of fourteen (1937–1950), and basic steel was down for a total of nine months in another fourteen-year period (1946–1959). Yet, production soared over the years both in these critical industries and in the economy as a whole. Even in the case of services, which cannot be stockpiled, consumers have adjusted to strikes in every form of public transportation and in nearly every type of public utility.

Second, these studies should induce a degree of humility in both critics and defenders of the strike, for they demonstrate how very difficult it is to estimate all the effects of a particular stoppage even when it is over and done with. Pity, then, the government official who must make such an estimate, and act upon it, while a strike is actually in progress.

But these studies have *not* answered the question of whether

[43]*ibid.*, p. 245.
[44]*ibid.*

emergency strikes are a rare or frequent event. One reason for this failure is that "emergency" inevitably means different things to different people. A dictionary definition of the word is "an unforeseen combination of circumstances which calls for immediate action"—a definition of no help whatever when the question is *which* strike circumstances "call for immediate action." Thus, everyone is free to define "emergency strike" pretty much as he pleases.

To the advocate of free collective bargaining, it is obvious that the government should take "immediate action" only in the direst of circumstances, and he will define emergency strikes accordingly: "immediate jeopardy to public health and safety," "serious harm to the economy," "a national crisis," "hardship rather than inconvenience," "dangerous curtailment of necessary services," phrases which pepper most of the case studies. By that kind of definition, as Warren observed of his own, "it may be seen that few strike situations *can* result in national emergencies during peacetime."[45] By the same token, strikes that only result in "severe economic losses"[46] or impose "inconveniences upon millions"[47] are not necessarily emergencies.

There are some minor divisions within this camp (Bernstein classed the 1952 steel strike as an emergency, for example, while Livernash did not), but on the whole these experts are agreed that very few, if any, strikes have ever created a true emergency in this country. Their evidence on this point is conclusive, provided you accept their definitions of an emergency.

On the other hand, to those less opposed to strike controls, such as Chamberlain and Schilling, the above definitions of an emergency are too restrictive:

> There is probably little to be gained and perhaps much to be lost by misleading ourselves into dismissing the strike problem as inconsequential on the ground that rarely has the public been forced to go hungry, rarely has it been permanently injured, rarely have

---

[45]Warren, p. 14, italics added.
[46]Kennedy, p. 19 and Warren, p. 14.
[47]Bernstein and Lovell, p. 365.

Emergency Strikes: Fact or Fancy?

> any lives been lost as a result of labor stoppages. Public policy is
> not commonly based on so Spartan a view. A general desire to keep
> government intervention to the minimum does not permit keeping
> it at less than the minimum which is publicly acceptable.[48]

These authors, it will be recalled, did not even attempt a definition of an emergency strike, believing it futile to search for any fixed line between the strikes warranting intervention and all others. Also, they emphasized the effects of strikes on producers as well as consumers, in sharp contrast to the Warren, Kennedy, and Livernash studies, which largely ignored the secondary unemployment effects of stoppages.

Which view is correct? Have the majority of case studies wished away the strike problem by defining emergencies as once-in-a-lifetime catastrophes? Or have Chamberlain and Schilling inflated the problem by quantifying every way in which every strike may remotely affect everybody? Surely no one can say that either approach is "wrong." That, in fact, is the key point: no matter how many statistics are amassed on the effects of any strike, they are meaningless until compared with some person's definition of an emergency. Yet, such a definition is often just a restatement of each person's opinion of whether the government should intervene in few or many strikes—although that is the question presumably being tested! In short, there is no definition of emergency strikes that is either scientifically objective or commonly accepted.

A second reason why these case studies are not conclusive is that many of them rest upon the extremely vulnerable assumption that, if past strikes have not created emergencies, this proves there is little need for the government to step into future strikes. This reasoning would be persuasive if there had been no government intervention in past strikes. If, for example, free collective bargaining had been the practice in steel over the past twenty years and no emergency strikes had resulted, then one could indeed argue that the government should stay out of future steel disputes.

---

[48]Chamberlain and Schilling, pp. 252–253.

National Emergency Strikes

As everyone knows, however, the government has repeatedly and vigorously intervened in past steel strikes, as well as in most of the coal and railroad and utility strikes examined by these studies. How, then, do you prove that the government should stop intervening in future strikes by showing that no emergencies developed when the government intervened in the past?

Conclusions

In one of his typical sallies, Russell Baker has suggested that strikes would bother no one if we had a U.S. Strike Forecast Bureau to issue helpful warnings such as this:

> Both air and sea travel warnings are posted for North America and large areas of Western Europe for the next six weeks. There is a 70 percent chance of extensive striking all along the United States airport front and a 90 percent chance of a general maritime strike in all British ports.
>
> A large mass of relative good-feeling prevailing over the bus drivers and the railroad brotherhoods indicates clear travel conditions by American road and rail through much of the summer....
>
> Illness warnings are flying over New York and San Francisco where persistent areas of low-salary have created a 50 percent chance of nurses' strikes during the next few weeks. Anyone in these areas anticipating an illness during this period is advised to postpone it until late summer when labor conditions will be more favorable for medical suffering.[49]

Unfortunately, we seem as unable to agree on the significance of yesterday's strikes as to predict the likelihood of tomorrow's. The emergency strike issue has been fought over for two decades now, and there is still no consensus on what an emergency strike is, or how many we have had in the past or are likely to have in the future. Most surprising, there have been fewer than ten serious studies of the impact of specific strikes, and only two in the last ten years.

It would be comforting if this fall-off in impact studies were

---

[49]Russell Baker, "How to Reduce the Strike Nuisance," *New York Times*, August 14, 1966, p. 10.

Emergency Strikes: Fact or Fancy?

a reflection of the decreasing importance of the issue itself, a development many predicted as imminent some years ago. It is true that strikes in some industries, such as coal and telephones, no longer are a cause for much public concern, nor did the world end when large-scale stoppages were recently permitted to occur in industries such as rubber, trucking, and copper. Yet, maritime and longshoring disputes are now as aggravating as coal strikes once were; other disputes, such as that in copper, are settled only by the informal but direct intervention of the President; compulsory arbitration has been invoked twice on the railroads; several strikes have been enjoined under Taft-Hartley—and in the summer of 1966, a congressional committee tried in vain to determine whether a month-long shutdown of 60 percent of the airline industry was or was not a national emergency.

Thus, the question of whether emergency strikes are fact or fiction refuses to fade away, nor is it likely to be answered conclusively in the near future. As Irving Bernstein has noted, "A really satisfying study would require a team of field researchers to examine exhaustively the effects of a particular strike while it was in progress."[50] Even then, we have seen, there would surely be disagreement over whether all these effects added up to a regrettable inconvenience or an intolerable emergency.

Meanwhile, the public and its representatives long ago decided that there were indeed emergency strikes and that something ought to be done about them before "that precise moment when the experts have concluded that...[a] stoppage is intolerable."[51] The results of that decision to do something are to be found in the stormy history of the Taft-Hartley and Railway Labor Acts.

---

[50]Bernstein, p. 26, n3.

[51]Harold L. Enarson, "The Politics of an Emergency Dispute: Steel, 1952," in Bernstein, Enarson, and Fleming, eds., *op. cit.*, p. 47.

III

Current Controls
on Emergency Strikes

MANY DISCUSSIONS IN THIS FIELD
leave the impression that strike controls are primarily creatures
of the postwar world, a response to the great growth in union
power since the 1930's. For better or for worse, however, the
government has actually been intervening in major labor
disputes for nearly a century, often using the same controls
being debated today.

Sometimes this intervention has been as blunt as sending in
federal troops, as in the railroad strikes of 1877, the country's
"first industrial outbreak on a national scale."[1] At other times,
the executive branch has gone to the courts for sweeping injunctions, as in the Pullman strike of 1894, the coal strike of
1919, and the rail strike of 1922. On the legislative front, Congress has been passing laws on and off since 1888 to cope with
railway labor disputes. And even White House "persuasion"
dates back to 1902, when President Theodore Roosevelt ended
an anthracite stoppage by secretly informing J. P. Morgan,

---

[1]Foster Rhea Dulles, *Labor in America* (New York: Thomas Y. Crowell
Co., 1955), p. 119.

"the real power behind the operators," that the government would seize the mines if the owners did not agree to arbitrate the dispute.[2] Half a century later, another coal strike was also ended promptly when President Truman asked Congress for authority to seize the mines. As historians keep reminding us, there is surprisingly little that is new under the sun.

Another common misconception is that the government must choose between doing nothing about strikes or passing a law to force the private parties to do something they don't want to do. There is, in fact, a third course that is available and has been pursued for many years: to encourage the use of mediation, a process in which skilled neutrals try to settle disputes by persuasion and ingenuity, not compulsion. There has been a federal mediation agency ever since 1917, and today nearly every state and several cities also provide some kind of mediation facilities.

Because mediation (or conciliation, which means the same) is a voluntary process, it is "the most frequent and, to the majority of persons, the most accepted form of government intervention in labor disputes."[3] The Federal Mediation and Conciliation Service, for example, currently participates in over seven thousand different negotiations each year, and the New York State Board of Mediation participates in over seven hundred a year. Also, at both the New York and federal levels, 90 percent or more of mediation cases are settled without strikes, although these cases probably involve a high proportion of the most difficult types of negotiation and of the large-scale disputes that most concern the public.[4]

Having said all this, we shall nevertheless ignore history and mediation in most of this chapter on strike controls. With

---

[2]*ibid.*, p. 193.

[3]Herbert R. Northrup and Gordon F. Bloom, *Government and Labor* (Homewood, Ill.: Richard D. Irwin, Inc., 1963), p. 273.

[4]*Federal Mediation and Conciliation Service, Eighteenth Annual Report, Fiscal Year 1965* (Washington: GPO, 1966), pp. 1–2 and *New York State Department of Labor, Annual Report, 1964*, vol. 2 (Albany, 1965), pp. 88 and 96.

respect to history, there have been such radical changes in labor relations over the years that few people would appraise a particular control today on the basis of how it worked around the turn of the century. Mediation, on the other hand, is certainly of current importance, but it has received so little systematic analysis that, for our purposes, one can do little more than define it and wish it well. Gross statistics on case loads, for example, do not really tell much about the effectiveness of this technique in the few, but critical, disputes in which both parties have great staying power and as much negotiating skill as the mediators.

Even when mediation does head off a large-scale strike, as it frequently appears to do, there is always the nagging question of whether it worked only because the parties knew the next step after "persuasion" would be compulsion of one sort or another. In other words, would this voluntary approach to dispute settlement prevent emergency strikes if it were not backed up by distasteful controls? On this and similar questions about mediation, there simply is little or no hard evidence available. In labor relations as elsewhere, it is always easier to describe the policeman's job than the displomat's.

For these reasons, we shall concentrate on those portions of the Taft-Hartley and Railway Labor Acts specifically designed to prevent national emergency strikes, reviewing their content, their performance records, and the many criticisms leveled at them.

The Taft-Hartley Act

The emergency strike controls that apply to most industries in the country are contained in Title II of the Labor-Management Relations (Taft-Hartley) Act of 1947. In brief, this section of the law provides, first, that if it is the President's opinion that a threatened or actual strike (or lockout), which affects "an entire industry or a substantial part thereof," will "imperil the national health or safety," he may appoint a "board of

53

inquiry" to investigate and report to him the facts of the dispute.

Second, upon receiving the board's report, the President may direct the Attorney General to petition the appropriate district court for an injunction, a court order forbidding the parties to begin or continue the stoppage in question. The court is empowered to issue such an order if it finds that the dispute meets the tests of industry coverage and peril to health and safety.

Third, if the court enjoins the stoppage, the parties must "make every effort" to settle their dispute voluntarily, with the help of the Federal Mediation and Conciliation Service. If no settlement has been reached after sixty days, the board of inquiry is to report to the President the then current positions of the parties and the efforts made at settlement, and this report is made public.

Fourth, within the next fifteen days, the National Labor Relations Board "shall take a secret ballot of the employees... on the question of whether they wish to accept the final offer of settlement made by their employer." The NLRB then has five more days in which to certify the results of this ballot to the Attorney General.

Finally, when the ballot results have been certified or a settlement has been reached, whichever happens sooner, the Attorney General must ask the court to end the injunction and the court must grant this request. The President is then directed to "submit to the Congress a full and comprehensive report of the proceedings . . . , together with such recommendations as he may see fit to make for consideration and appropriate action."

In effect, then, the law enables the President to delay a critical strike for eighty days, during which it is hoped that the parties will settle voluntarily. If they do not settle, a strike may legally occur after the eighty-day period, unless Congress chooses to enact some additional controls.

The Record of 20 Years

Table 6 summarizes some of the salient aspects of Taft-Hartley's performance in emergency disputes during the first two decades this law has been in effect. No one, of course, believes that such a simple box score is an adequate basis for judging any law, much less one as complex as this. No table can measure the fairness of an injunction, for example, or its effect on the quality of negotiations, and even those facts included in the table are open to different interpretations, as we shall soon see. Facts are in such short supply in this field, however, that the few available deserve examination.

Looking first at the industries in which the emergency provisions have been applied, it is obvious that longshoring and ocean shipping long ago replaced Mr. Lewis and his coal miners as the prime target area for Title II injunctions. Not only have these two related industries been involved in nine of the twenty-four injunction cases, but they account for *all seven* of the strikes which occurred after the act's procedures were exhausted. Rehmus has suggested that this sad record is a result of bitter interunion rivalries over a "limited and declining number of jobs" in these industries, almost equally serious divisions among the several employer groups, and union-management hostility dating back to the violent organizing years.[5]

The act has also been invoked a total of twelve times in direct defense industries: five times in atomic energy (counting case 10),[6] twice in aerospace, once in aircraft manufacturing, and, following the build-up in Vietnam, three times in plants producing military aircraft engines and once in shipbuilding. This pattern indicates again how difficult it is today to dis-

---

[5]Charles M. Rehmus, "Taft-Hartley Title II: An Emergency at Sea," *Labor Law Journal*, vol. 14, no. 10 (October 1963), p. 870.

[6]For an account of the labor problems peculiar to the atomic energy industry and the special machinery created to handle its threatened work stoppages, see Robert C. Crawford, "Government Intervention in Emergency Labor Disputes in Atomic Energy," *Labor Law Journal*, vol. 10, no. 6 (June 1959), pp. 414–434.

Table 6. The Taft-Hartley Act's Record in National Emergency Disputes, 1947–1967.

Industry and date of dispute	Injunction issued?	Strike in progress before injunction?	Strike halted by injunction?	Settlement reached during or after injunction period?	Any strike after injunction period?	Result of last-offer ballot
1. Atomic energy, 1948............	Yes	No	—	After	No	Reject
2. Meatpacking, 1948............	No	—	—	—	—	—
3. Bituminous coal, 1948............	Yes	Yes	Yes*	During	—	—
4. Telephone, 1948............	No	—	—	—	—	—
5. Maritime (all coasts), 1948............	Yes	No	—	Both†	Yes†	Reject‡
6. Bituminous coal, 1948............	No	—	—	—	—	—
7. Longshoring, Atlantic coast, 1948	Yes	No	—	After	Yes	Reject
8. Bituminous coal, 1949–1950......	Yes	Yes	No§	During§	—	—
9. Nonferrous metals, 1951	Yes	Yes	Yes	During	—	Reject
10. Fabricated steel‖ and atomic energy, 1952¶............	Yes	Yes	Yes	During	—	—
11. Longshoring, Atlantic coast, 1953	Yes	Yes	Yes	After**	Yes**	**
12. Atomic energy, 1954............	Yes	Yes††	Yes††	After	No	Reject
13. Atomic energy, 1954............	No	—	—	—	—	—
14. Longshoring, Atlantic and Gulf coasts, 1956–1957............	Yes	Yes	Yes	After	Yes	Reject
15. Atomic energy, 1957............	Yes	Yes	Yes	After	No	Reject

Industry and date of dispute	Injunction issued?	Strike in progress before injunction?	Strike Halted by Injunction?	Settlement reached during or after injunction period?	Any strike after injunction period?	Result of last-offer ballot
16. Longshoring, Atlantic and Gulf coasts, 1959	Yes	Yes	Yes	During	—	Reject
17. Basic steel, 1959	Yes	Yes	Yes	During	—	Reject
18. Maritime (all coasts), 1961	Yes	Yes	Yes	Both‡‡	Yes‡‡	Reject
19. Maritime, West coast, 1962	Yes	Yes	Yes	During	—	—
20. Aircraft manufacturing, 1962¶	Yes	Yes	Yes	During	—	—
21. Longshoring, Atlantic and Gulf coasts, 1962–1963	Yes	Yes	Yes	After	Yes	Reject
22. Aerospace, 1962	Yes	Yes	Yes§§	During	—	—
23. Aerospace, 1962–1963	Yes	No	—	After	No	Reject
24. Longshoring, Atlantic and Gulf coasts, 1964–1965	Yes	Yes	Yes	After	Yes	—
25. Military aircraft engines, 1966.¶	Yes	Yes	Yes	During	—	—
26. Military aircraft engines, 1966.¶	Yes	Yes	Yes	During	—	—
27. West coast shipyards, 1967	Yes	Yes	Yes	Both‖‖	No	—‖‖
28. Military aircraft engines, 1967.¶	Yes	Yes	Yes	During	—	—

Sources: U.S. Bureau of Labor Statistics, *National Emergency Disputes Under the Labor Management Relations (Taft-Hartley) Act, 1947–65*, Bulletin no. 1482 (Washington: GPO, 1966); Federal Mediation and Conciliation Service, *20th Anniversary Report, 1947–1967* (Washington: GPO, 1967), pp. 12–29; and various issues of the *Monthly Labor Review*.

Notes to Table 6:

*A temporary restraining order (in effect, an injunction) was issued on April 3, 1949. When the strike continued, the court found John L. Lewis and the United Mine Workers of America guilty of contempt of court and fined Lewis $20,000 and the union $1,400,000. Most of the strikers returned to work on April 24–26. Thus, the strike was halted by the injunction, but only after three weeks.

†This complex dispute involved six shipping unions on all the coasts, plus the longshoremen's union on the West coast. Agreements were reached during and just after the injunction period on the Atlantic and Gulf coasts and on the Great Lakes, but a three-month strike ensued on the West coast before agreement was reached.

‡The International Longshoremen's and Warehousemen's Union boycotted the balloting on the employers' last offer and not a single vote was cast in its jurisdiction. Members of the other West coast unions involved received ballots by mail, but the NLRB was unable to complete its balloting of off-shore personnel before the injunction expired.

§Temporary restraining order issued on February 11, 1950; miners refused to return to work; contempt proceedings again initiated against union, but UMWA found not guilty of ordering the strike continued; President Truman asked Congress on March 3 for authority to seize the mines; agreement reached on March 5.

‖This dispute is classified in the fabricated steel industry because it occurred in the American Locomotive Company's plant at Dunkirk, N.Y. The basis of government intervention, however, was that the plant was the source of parts deemed essential to the atomic energy industry.

¶Each of these disputes was confined to a single plant or company: an American Locomotive plant (case 10); the Republic Aviation Corporation in Farmingdale, Long Island (case 20); a General Electric plant in Evandale, Ohio, which produced jet engines for planes used in Vietnam (case 25); a Union Carbide plant in Kokomo, Indiana, which produced alloys and parts for jet engines (case 26); and an AVCO Corporation plant in Stratford, Connecticut, which was the sole supplier of engines for certain types of helicopters used in Vietnam (case 28).

**Although this dispute began in October 1953 over the terms of a new contract, it quickly became a year-long battle over which of two unions would represent the longshoremen in the Port of New York. The NLRB cancelled the scheduled referendum on the employers' last offer; the injunction expired; stoppages occurred over the representation issue; and a new contract was not negotiated until December 1954.

†Board of inquiry was appointed on July 6, 1954; strike began on July 7; board reported to President and strike halted voluntarily on July 10; injunction obtained August 11 to avert a threatened resumption of the strike.

‡‡Six of the seven unions involved settled with shipowners during the period of the injunction. A strike by the seventh union began in Pacific coast ports on September 28; by October 4, 28 ships were tied up; settlement was reached October 11.

§§The strike was actually halted, at the request of mediators, as soon as the board of inquiry was appointed, five days before the injunction was issued.

‖‖In this unusual dispute, the parties settled a number of issues both before and during the injunction period, and also agreed to submit unresolved issues to the members of the board of inquiry for fact-finding and recommendations if necessary, to extend the no-strike period beyond the 80-day limit of the injunction, and to have the NLRB supervise a last-offer ballot before any strike action would be taken. As a result, the board actively mediated, a full settlement was reached during the voluntary no-strike period after the injunction had expired, and the union members ratified this agreement in an NLRB-conducted ballot. Since the union negotiators had agreed to the settlement terms, however, this ballot was not the same as that required by the act, in which union members are asked to vote on an employer's offer that has been rejected by their officers.

tinguish between peacetime and wartime settings in discussing emergency strikes. In fact, the government can and frequently does cite the defense impact of stoppages in other industries, such as steel, in seeking injunctive relief. Finally, speaking of steel, note that it has been the subject of only one Title II case (in 1959), although steel strikes have been frequent and have precipitated nearly every other kind of government intervention.

From the dates of these cases, it can be seen that President Truman invoked the act's emergency provision ten times in five years, President Eisenhower seven times in eight years, President Kennedy six times in three years, and President Johnson five times in his first four years in office (through 1967). There has been almost no speculation as to what political significance, if any, can be read into these figures. Why, for example, was the law used far more frequently by President Truman, who had vetoed the original bill and strongly criticized its emergency provisions and was supposedly prolabor, than by President Eisenhower, who essentially approved of the law and was labeled promanagement? Was the Eisenhower record a vindication of the policy of minimizing government intervention in the economy, or was the labor front relatively quiet in those years for other reasons?

The other columns are largely self-explanatory. Of the twenty strikes in progress before a Title II injunction was secured, only two (cases 3 and 8) continued in the face of the court order, and one of these was halted after three weeks when the union and its president were fined for contempt of court. Also, of the twenty-four disputes that were enjoined, seventeen were settled without further strikes, and in two of the others, both maritime disputes that originally involved all coasts, peaceful settlements were reached on all coasts but the Pacific (cases 5 and 18). By these pragmatic tests, the Taft-Hartley's emergency provisions come off quite well: in the disputes deemed serious enough to merit an injunction, strikes in progress were halted nearly every time and peaceful settlements were achieved in about three out of every four cases (the exact score depending on how you count the partial settlements in cases 5 and 18).

On the other side of the ledger, the act *did* fail to stop strikes in eight of the twenty-four injunction cases—the third coal case, in which the original strike continued until President Truman threatened seizure, and the seven maritime cases, in which postinjunction strikes occurred. Nor were these trivial failures, for among the postinjunction strikes were a three-month shutdown of Pacific Coast shipping (case 5) and several total or partial shutdowns of East Coast ports, ranging in length from ten days (case 14) to two months (case 24).

Finally, note the spotless record rolled up by the last-offer ballot. In 1947, Congress inserted this ballot provision in the belief that union officials frequently did not represent their members' wishes and, if given a choice, the members would often prefer to take their employer's last offer rather than strike.[7] As Table 6 indicates, however, the workers have rejected management's last offer in every secret poll conducted by the government under Title II of Taft-Hartley.

Criticisms of the Act

Statistics settle very few arguments in labor relations, and certainly the handful that can be gleaned from Table 6 have had no perceptible effect on the controversy surrounding Title II. Since these emergency strike provisions have provoked more criticism than any other section of the Taft-Hartley Act (with the possible exception of its union security provisions), the following discussion can do no more than summarize the major attacks upon Title II and the responses made to them.[8]

---

[7]It should be noted that the law does not make the results of the last-offer ballot binding upon union officials. It was anticipated, however, that union officials would be reluctant to call a strike in the face of a poll showing that their members preferred to accept the employer's last offer.

[8]Of the several relevant sources already cited in this and preceding chapters, see in particular Irving Bernstein, Harold L. Enarson, and R. W. Fleming, eds., *Emergency Disputes and National Policy* (New York: Harper and Brothers, 1955), which remains probably the single best source

National Emergency Strikes

1. The most basic criticism, of course, is that there have been few if any labor disputes requiring more than mediation by the government, and certainly there have not been twenty-four that have merited injunctions since 1947. The pros and cons of this charge have already been discussed in Chapter II and need not be reviewed here.

2. If the government must intervene, however, critics view the injunction as a one-sided weapon to use. The injunction is particularly offensive to labor because of its sordid history as a union-busting device before the 1930's, and because its use implies that only labor, and never management, is responsible for a breakdown in negotiations. Also, when the injunction takes effect, workers must continue to work under the old wage scale and other working conditions they want changed, while management has eighty more days of production and profit on the terms of the contract that has already expired.[9] This, it

in this field. Other relevant sources not previously cited include George W. Taylor, "The Adequacy of Taft-Hartley in Public Emergency Disputes," *Annals of the American Academy of Political and Social Science,* vol. 333, January 1961, pp. 76–84; John Perry Horlacher, "A Political Science View of National Emergency Disputes," in *ibid.,* pp. 85–95; Archibald Cox, *Law and National Labor Policy* (University of California at Los Angeles, Institute of Industrial Relations, 1960); David L. Cole, *The Quest for Industrial Peace* (New York: McGraw-Hill, 1963); Alfred Giardino, "National Emergency Strike Legislation" in *New York University Sixteenth Annual Conference on Labor* (New York: Matthew Bender, 1963), pp. 233–250; Louis Waldman, "National Emergency Strikes: The Need for New Procedures and Devices" in *ibid.,* pp. 251–272; James E. Jones, Jr., "The National Emergency Disputes Provisions of the Taft-Hartley Act: A View from a Legislative Draftsman's Desk," *Western Reserve Law Review,* vol. 17, no. 1 (October 1965), pp. 133–256; and Arthur A. Sloane, "Presidential Boards of Inquiry in National Emergency Disputes, An Assessment after 20 Years of Performance," *Labor Law Journal,* November 1967, pp. 665–675.

[9] An interesting legal question is whether a district court has the power to order management to make any subsequent wage and fringe-benefit increases retroactive to the date the injunction was issued, thus reducing labor's disadvantage. In only one instance (case 14 in Table 6) has a court issued such an order. In another (case 16), the judge specifically denied a union request for retroactivity, and in another (case 17), the issue was

is charged, is neither an equitable nor an effective way of inducing an agreement, for it places no pressure whatever upon management for most of the injunction period.

Defenders of the act retort that most of the union-busting injunctions of former days were secured by employers from conservative judges with no statutory guidance, and that Taft-Hartley injunctions can be obtained only by the government and under conditions stipulated in the act. As for the unequal effect of an injunction on the parties' bargaining postures, the same could be said of other strike controls sometimes preferred to the injunction. When the government slaps a "paper seizure" on a company and takes it over in name only, for example, or when, under the Railway Labor Act, a Presidential request is enough to stop a strike, the bargaining effects are precisely the same as under an injunction: the workers are working on the old terms for a management making its pre-strike profits.

3. Alternatively, it is often argued that the injunction fails because it relieves *both* parties of any pressure to engage in honest bargaining. In effect, it is said, the strike deadline that precipitates most agreements is just moved back eighty days; instead of this being a cooling-off period during which mediation and second thoughts can prevail, it becomes a "warming-up period" for the next deadline. At this point, the critics point to the twelve disputes that were not settled (in whole or in part) until after Title II injunctions expired, while others argue that the timing of settlements is less important than the fact that they were reached peacefully in a clear majority of the cases.

4. It has also been charged that Title II betrays a peculiar logic in first declaring that certain strikes threaten the nation's very health and safety and then blithely proceeding to permit such strikes after a mere eighty days, unless the entire Congress is hauled into the case. Closely allied to this attack is another

---

extensively argued but never resolved by the court. In most cases, however, injunctions have, in effect, required that preinjunction terms and conditions of employment be maintained.

already mentioned, namely, that the act has flunked its most basic test by not stopping several of the strikes declared to be emergencies since 1947.

To these charges, the answer is offered that if Congress had intended to outlaw these strikes it would have adopted one of the more extreme weapons, such as compulsory arbitration, which are criticized even more than the temporary injunction. The aim was instead to impose a limited cooling-off period, in the hope that that would be enough. If it were not, the door was left open for Congress to adopt more extreme measures in a critical situation—but it would have been a mistake to spell these measures out beforehand, for they might then have been used as a matter of course. As for the act's failures to stop every strike to which it has been applied, the reply is that no strike control has a perfect record in this respect. (Note how the players switch roles here, with the critics in effect arguing that the law is not tough enough and the defense urging moderation in restricting labor's right to strike.)

5. It is frequently argued that the act's emergency provisions are so inflexible, and thus predictable, that bargaining in key situations inevitably tends to adjust to the next foreseeable legal step, rather than centering upon the issues in dispute. If either party wants a helping hand from Washington, it knows just how to get it, this argument runs, and once the Title II machinery is set in motion, everyone in the country knows what is coming next at every stage.

If there must be intervention, this view holds, let its nature and timing be as unpredictable as possible. If the President can choose among several weapons, such as seizure and fact-finding and compulsory arbitration, as well as the injunction or just doing nothing, perhaps then both parties will be so apprehensive about his choice that they will prefer to settle their dispute by themselves. Also, it is said, this approach would permit the President to select the tactic most suitable to a particular dispute, in contrast to the Taft-Hartley's implication that the same technique is equally apt for all situations.

The defense offers three rebuttals to this criticism: the last step in Title II's provisions, suggesting that Congress may legislate further in any dispute still unsettled, introduces precisely the uncertainty (if not sheer terror) that critics are looking for; no matter how many weapons in a President's armory, the politics of each situation will pretty clearly tell the parties beforehand which one he will use; and, finally, all four Presidents in the 1947–1967 period felt free to use other tactics in addition to Taft-Hartley, as the varied history of steel disputes alone will show.

6. Impartial observers are nearly unanimous in urging that the present act should be amended to grant the boards of inquiry the power, in their discretion, to make recommendations for settling disputes. Since the law now specifically prohibits the boards from making such recommendations, it is said that their reports offer no point around which public opinion can mobilize, and board members, who are typically chosen from the most skilled neutrals in the field, are largely wasted on reportorial functions. This change was agreed to by both Senator Taft, in his proposed amendments in 1949, and by President Eisenhower, in his 1954 proposals, but the law remains unchanged on this point as on all others.

Needless to say, agreement is by no means universal on the need for such a change. One of the reasons for the law's restriction on the boards of inquiry is that many employers in 1947 believed that so-called neutrals were often prounion in their sympathies, and this feeling is certainly not extinct today. Further, a persuasive argument can be made that this single change in the law could convert the emergency provisions into something very close to compulsory arbitration. In any large-scale dispute, it is said, the pressures from the White House and Congress for a peaceful settlement may now be intense but they are relatively unfocused. Given a set of terms recommended by neutrals, however, this pressure would inevitably be drawn toward forcing the parties to settle at or near those terms, in which case the line between "recommendations" and a compulsory arbitration award can become very thin indeed. (We shall return to this point in our discussion of the Railway Labor Act, under which neutral boards have regularly offered recommendations.)

7. Finally, there is also widespread agreement that the ballot on the employer's last offer is futile and should be dropped. This is not because workers love to strike, but rather, as most experts see it, that such a ballot unavoidably becomes a vote of confidence in the union leadership, which has recommended that management's last offer be rejected. Further, when the employer knows his last offer will be rejected and that the union negotiators will be back for more, he may well keep something in reserve when he states his nominal last offer for the NLRB balloting; but the union negotiators suspect the employer is holding back for these reasons, whether he is or not, so this reinforces their belief that more can be had; and so on and on, in a cat-and-mouse game that can seriously complicate bargaining during the injunction period.[10]

To others, however, the principle of offering workers a chance to vote on this question is so important that it little matters how the balloting actually turns out.

The Railway Labor Act

In the light of these many criticisms of Taft-Hartley, the Railway Labor Act presents a particularly interesting contrast in the control of emergency strikes. Before being adopted by

---

[10]In the middle of the 1966 airlines strike, the Machinists union created consternation by announcing that it was recessing negotiations for a week in order to poll its members on whether or not to accept the employers' latest offer, although the governing Railway Labor Act does not require any such poll. Government mediators argued that everyone knew what the vote would be, since the union officials were not recommending acceptance, and finally persuaded the union to abandon its voting plan and to get on with the bargaining!

Current Controls on Emergency Strikes

Congress, the basic elements of this law were first worked out between the union and management groups who would have to live with it, a procedure sometimes urged for amending Taft-Hartley. Also, the railway law was drafted in the relatively peaceful years of the mid-1920's, rather than in a period of public hysteria over strikes, which is how many view the postwar setting of the Taft-Hartley Act. Further, the Railway Labor Act emphasizes mediation and voluntary arbitration, has been interpreted to permit recommendations by neutral boards, and does not call for either injunctions or last-offer ballots.

More specifically, the Railway Labor Act of 1926, as amended, provides for a National Mediation Board to assist in resolving labor disputes in both the railroad and airlines industries. If the private parties in these industries cannot settle a dispute themselves, either one may call in the Mediation Board, or it may volunteer its services "in case any labor emergency is found by it to exist at any time."

When the Board comes into a dispute, its mandate is first to "use its best efforts" to obtain an agreement by mediation. If mediation fails, the Board is instructed to try "to induce the parties to submit their controversy to arbitration." If the patries refuse to arbitrate, the NMB notifies them in writing that mediation has failed, and for the next thirty days "no change shall be made" unilaterally in wages or working conditions, a polite way of saying no strike shall occur.

At any point in this thirty-day period, if the Mediation Board believes that a dispute "threaten[s] substantially to interrupt interstate commerce to a degree such as to deprive any section of the country of essential transportation service," it so notifies the President, who may "create a board to investigate and report respecting such dispute." The emergency board is to report to the President within thirty days from the date of its creation. During these thirty days, and "for thirty days after such board has made its report to the President, no change, except by agreement, shall be made by the parties...in the conditions out of which the dispute arose."

67

National Emergency Strikes

Thus, like Taft-Hartley, the Railway Labor Act provides the President with a method for postponing a major strike temporarily, in this case for sixty to ninety days, during which time it is hoped that the parties will settle voluntarily. If they do not settle, the act is silent as to what further action, if any, the government may take. Note again the emphasis on voluntary agreement, not only in settling disputes, but also in complying with the law itself. Its various provisions simply tell the parties when they should not take unilateral action, without any mention of court orders or penalties for noncompliance. Also, although the act neither directs nor (as Taft-Hartley does) forbids the emergency boards to make recommendations, in practice nearly every board has offered its proposed solution to the dispute before it.

The Record of 41 Years

It is even more difficult to quantify the emergency strike record of the Railway Labor Act than that of Taft-Hartley, but Table 7 at least provides a basis for discussion. It clearly shows, for example, why this act achieved a reputation as the model labor law in the 1920's and 1930's—and also suggests some of the reasons why it has since been branded as a near disaster.

In retrospect, it has been suggested that this law looked so good in the 1930's partly because labor relations in the rest of the economy looked so bad.[11] This was the period when organizing strikes seemed to be occurring everywhere, but this battle had been fought and won by railway unions many years before. In fact, bargaining was so well established on the railroads that management itself had instituted industry-wide bargaining in 1932, in order to negotiate a 10 percent wage cut. It is true

---

[11]Herbert R. Northrup, "Emergency Disputes under the Railway Labor Act," *Proceedings of the First Annual Meeting, Industrial Relations Research Association* (IRRA, 1948), pp. 80–81; and Jacob J. Kaufman, *Collective Bargaining in the Railroad Industry* (New York: King's Crown Press, 1954), pp. 78–80.

that organizing was then taking place in the airlines (which came under the act in 1936), but the strongest union, that of the pilots, was gaining more through legislation in this period than through collective bargaining.[12]

In spite of the upturn in the number of strikes and emergency boards after 1940, however, the strike record in Table 7 is remarkably good in many respects. In the railroad industry alone, there were about a million employees through much of this period, a majority of them union members, and the number of railway labor contracts in force rose from three thousand in 1935 to over five thousand today.[13] In addition, there are twenty-two unions in this industry, several of them bitter rivals for jobs and members; employment has plummeted by 50 percent since 1945; and the industry has been beset by a host of competitive difficulties. Given all this potential for labor disputes, even the post-1940 strike record looks very good indeed: ten to twenty strikes a year, usually involving only a few thousand workers. In fact, there have been only two nationwide strikes on the rails in all these years, one in 1946 and the other in 1967, and each lasted only two days. Thus, the proportion of work time lost in strikes has been even lower in this industry than in the private economy as a whole.[14]

Also, it must be remembered that the strike data in Table 7 refer to *all* work stoppages in these two industries, and not just to those considered emergency disputes. How effective has the act been in preventing strikes in the emergency category? First, there have been very few strikes *during* the sixty-day cooling-off period following the appointment of an emergency board, even though the act prescribes no injunction or penal-

[12]Charles M. Mason, "Collective Bargaining Structure: The Airlines Experience" in Arnold R. Weber, ed., *The Structure of Collective Bargaining* (New York: The Free Press of Glencoe, 1961), pp. 220–221.

[13]National Mediation Board, *Thirty-First Annual Report*, for the fiscal year ended June 30, 1965 (Washington: GPO, 1966), Table 8, p. 75.

[14]Kaufman, pp. 79–80.

National Emergency Strikes

Table 7. Strikes and Emergency Boards in the Railroad and Airline Industries, 1926–1967.

Year*	Number of Emergency Boards Appointed†		Number of Strikes		Number of Workers Involved in Strikes	
	Rail	Air‡	Rail	Air	Rail	Air
1926......	–	–	n.a.	n.a.	–	–
1927......	–	–	–	–	–	–
1928......	1	–	1	–	7,000	–
1929......	2	–	3	–	396	–
1930......	–	–	1	–	106	–
1931......	1	–	–	–	–	–
1932......	1	–	–	1	–	23
1933......	1	–	–	1	–	21
1934......	5	–	–	–	–	–
1935......	–	–	1	1	28	69
1936......	1	–	2	–	587	–
1937......	3	–	6	–	1,095	–
1938......	1	–	1	–	25	–
1939......	1	–	–	2	–	128
1940......	–	–	1	–	71	–
1941......	4	–	5	–	1,163	–
1942......	2	–	9	–	1,340	–
1943......	11	–	8	1	3,269	35
1944......	2	–	12	–	3,244	–
1945......	27	3	13	2	5,790	2,690
1946......	19	1	17	2	356,000	14,700
1947......	21	1	7	2	13,900	1,520
1948......	15	1	12	3	3,670	1,760
1949......	10	2	10	3	49,700	420
1950......	11	–	17	3	261,000	8,280
1951......	6	2	17	5	75,900	6,670
1952......	4	2	15	7	48,500	2,450
1953......	1	3	23	7	15,600	3,830
1954......	2	–	10	4	3,910	3,480
1955......	2	1	20	7	40,200	990
1956......	5	–	14	3	7,200	1,580
1957......	3	–	15	2	16,600	2,990
1958......	1	5	11	18	3,300	45,300
1959......	–	1	10	6	7,780	5,290
1960......	6	1	16	12	101,000	18,300
1961......	3	2	9	6	24,300	77,600

Table 7 (continued)

1962......	6	6	4	1	15,700	17,100
1963......	3	1	8	9	3,040	5,490
1964......	4	2	27	15	46,000	14,100
1965......	4	–	19	7	46,800	17,700
1966......	1	1	n.a.	n.a.	n.a.	n.a.
1967......	2	2	n.a.	n.a.	n.a.	n.a.

Sources: Emergency board data for 1926–1934 from U.S. Bureau of Labor Statistics, Handbook of Labor Statistics, 1931 ed. (Bulletin 541), p. 13 and 1936 ed. (Bulletin 616), pp. 21–26; and from Annual Reports of the U.S. Board of Mediation. Data for 1935–1967 from Annual Reports of the National Mediation Board. Strike data for 1927–1936 from Florence Peterson, Strikes in the United States, 1880–1936, U.S. Bureau of Labor Statistics, Bulletin 651 (Washington: GPO, 1938), Table 37, pp. 154–155. Data for other years from BLS annual reports on work stoppages.

*Board data are for the fiscal years ending June 30; strike data are for calendar years.

†Includes all boards appointed under section 10 of the Railway Labor Act, including those appointed in 1943–1947 from the National Railway Labor Panel, a wartime device established by Executive Order to supplement the procedures of section 10. For reasons which are not clear, the totals for 1934–1947 in this table, although based on an examination of each of the annual reports of the NMB, do not tally precisely with that agency's announced totals of 170 boards in those years, plus 58 panel boards in 1943–1947. The comparable figures used in this table are 167 and 52.

‡The airlines were not covered by the act until April 1936.

ties against such strikes. In fact, this study uncovered only one such strike, a six-hour stoppage on the Southern Pacific in 1947;[15] if there have been others, they have not been of major consequence. As for strikes following the final reports of emergency boards, no study has been made of the entire 1926–1967 period, but during the fiscal years 1948–1967, there were 121 boards appointed and only 16 strikes occurred after these

---

[15]National Mediation Board, Fourteenth Annual Report, for the fiscal year ended June 30, 1948 (Washington: GPO, 1948), p. 45.

boards reported.[16] During the same years, it will be recalled, there were 24 Title II injunctions issued under the Taft-Hartley Act and 7 postinjunction strikes.

Finally, in a summary of its operations from 1934 to 1957, the National Mediation Board claimed over three thousand mediated settlements in those years and a total of 176 disputes settled by voluntary arbitration.[17]

All in all, the statistical record suggests that the Railway Labor Act has performed about as well as can be expected of any emergency strike law. Why, then, does it have so few friends and admirers?

Criticisms of the Act

In the opinion of nearly every scholar who has written on this subject, the statistics above create a totally misleading picture of how the Railway Labor Act has actually fared in major disputes, particularly in the years since 1940. Not only has this law made a shambles of the bargaining process on the railroads, say the critics, but it cannot even claim credit for the absence of major rail and air strikes during most of these years.

Many date the critical turning point in the act's history as November of 1941. Earlier that year, all of the railroad unions had asked for wage increases and management had countered with demands that certain work rules be changed to eliminate alleged featherbedding. When private negotiations reached an impasse, the law's emergency machinery went into action: first, mediation failed to produce a settlement; next, management accepted the suggestion of voluntary arbitration, but the unions rejected it; then, an emergency board was appointed and made

---

[16]Strike figures are from Orme Phelps, "Compulsory Arbitration: Some Perspectives," *Industrial and Labor Relations Review*, vol. 18, no. 1 (October 1964), p. 85; and *Annual Reports* of the National Mediation Board for 1963–1967.

[17]National Mediation Board, *Administration of the Railway Labor Act by the National Mediation Board, 1934–1957* (Washington: GPO, 1958), p. 45.

recommendations which management accepted but the unions rejected, and a nationwide strike was scheduled for early December 1941, at the end of the thirty-day period following the issuance of the emergency board's report.

At this point, President Roosevelt asked for further negotiations and, when these failed, took the unprecedented step of reconvening the emergency board and suggesting that it reappraise its original recommendations. Taking the hint, the board acted directly as a mediation panel and, shortly before the strike deadline, produced an agreement on terms well above its original recommendations. The key operating group (engineers, firemen, etc.) received a 10½ percent increase, in contrast to the 7½ percent first recommended; the "non-ops" received 10 cents instead of the 9 recommended; and no changes were made in work rules.

This was the pattern that became all too familiar in succeeding years in major rail disputes, with management accepting board recommendations and labor frequently winning more by threatening to strike and thus inducing White House intervention.[18] Critics say that this pattern represents a complete breakdown of the act, and that "peace-at-any-price" settlements, won after all the act's procedures have failed, can not be termed victories just because few strikes actually occur. Defenders of the law insist that "in most instances the recommendations of the boards have been accepted by the parties as a basis for resolving their disputes without resorting to a final test of economic strength,"[19] and that this is all the act intends. In this view, if board recommendations must be accepted to the penny and in every case, then there would be no difference between this law and compulsory arbitration.

Also, the strike figures in Table 7 do not reveal that, in

---

[18]Northrup, *loc cit.;* Kaufman, *loc cit.;* and David M. Levinson, "Railway Labor Act—the Record of a Decade," *Labor Law Journal,* vol. 3, no. 1 (January 1952), pp. 13–29.

[19]National Mediation Board, *Thirty-First Annual Report,* for the fiscal year ended June 30, 1965 (Washington: GPO, 1966), p. 7.

several of the major rail disputes of the past twenty-five years, strikes were stopped or averted only when strong measures were taken after the act's machinery had failed. In 1943, President Roosevelt seized the railroads and personally arbitrated a dispute that two boards had failed to settle. In 1946, President Truman seized the roads and a strike still occurred, with settlement reached only as the President was asking Congress for authority to draft the strikers, to strip them of their seniority rights, and to permit the government to set the workers' wages and retain the companies' profits during the period of seizure. In 1948 and again in 1950, both seizure and injunctions were used to head off rail strikes and, in the winter of 1950–1951, the Trainmen's union was twice fined for violating one of these injunctions.

As Table 7 shows, there were few boards or major strikes in the 1950's,[20] but when the work rules issue finally came to a head in the early 1960's Congress prevented a rail stoppage with the first compulsory arbitration law ever passed in peacetime on the national level. Finally, in the 1967 wage dispute between six shopcraft unions and most of the major rail lines, this bizarre sequence of events occurred: the unions rejected the emergency board's recommendations; at the President's request Congress passed a special law extending the normal 30-day no-strike period for another 20 days; the President appointed a new special mediation panel, whose recommendations were rejected by the unions; Congress passed another law extending the no-strike period, this time for another 47 days; at the end of that time, the unions struck for 2 days and Congress passed a third law, ordering the men back to work and setting up a

---

[20]Northrup and Bloom, p. 325, suggest that this slackening of activity in the 1950's resulted from the unions' knowledge that they could not count on favorable intervention from President Eisenhower. Kaufman suggests that the slackening resulted partly from labor's reluctance to have emergency boards pass on the carriers' increasingly insistent demands for changes in alleged featherbedding rules. Jacob J. Kaufman, "Emergency Boards under the Railway Labor Act," *Labor Law Journal*, vol. 9, no. 12 (December 1958), pp. 913–914.

third board to decide the issues. (Although the Administration delicately termed this last step "mediation to finality," few observers could discern how it differed from compulsory arbitration.)

Faced with this record of massive intervention, ask the critics, how can anyone credit the voluntarism of the Railway Labor Act for the absence of major rail strikes?[21]

The final count in the indictment against the act is that it has largely paralyzed the bargaining process in major disputes. Since both parties are said to expect these cases inevitably to go to emergency boards and perhaps then to the White House, neither has an incentive to settle voluntarily in private negotiations or in the mediation sessions that must precede the appointment of a board. The most extreme example of the delays that can result in this setting is that of the rail dispute over the use of diesel firemen and other working rules. This case went through a Presidential Commission, then a "normal" emergency board, and then a special committee appointed by the President, in addition to a Supreme Court case, mediation by the Secretary of Labor, deadline extensions requested by the President and then by congressional leaders, hearings before House and Senate committees, and finally the proceedings of the arbitration board ordered by Congress. Initiated on November 2, 1959, this case was finally decided by the arbitrators on November 26, 1963, and their award was in turn upheld by the courts on April 27, 1964.[22]

As for the parties' behavior before emergency boards, one experienced neutral has recently termed board procedures "increasingly formal, cumbersome, expensive and unproductive."

> The ritual of presenting the case to the board is as stylized as the courtship dance of the great crested grebe. The board, immobilized by hours of hearings during which prepared testimony is literally

---

[21]For a review of the airlines' experience under the act, see Mason, pp. 217–255.

[22]Jacob J. Kaufman, "The Railroad Labor Dispute: A Marathon of Maneuver and Improvisation," *Industrial and Labor Relations Review,* vol. 18, no. 2 (January 1965), pp. 197–200.

read into the record, and smothered by an avalanche of printed exhibits and briefs, has no time for open, forthright mediation.... Genuine collective bargaining seldom begins until after the board's report and recommendations have been released.[23]

Rather surprisingly, this observer added that the board recommendations "nevertheless...have usually provided the basis for the eventual settlement."[24]

In closing, it is interesting to note that, in a recent panel discussion of the Railway Labor Act, three of the four independent experts spoke critically of the law, but both the management and union representatives defended it. The management spokesman contended that the act's board procedures had a good record in light of the many problems faced by the industry, and a consultant to rail unions stated that the major problems lay not with the act's procedures but with the experts themselves, who frequently serve as board members but who, he charged, really had little knowledge of the railroad industry.[25]

Conclusions

If the emergency provisions of the Taft-Hartley and Railway Labor Acts are even half as bad as the weight of expert opinion holds, why have they not been scrapped or, at least, substantially amended? Probably one reason is the rough balance of political power that has existed in recent years between labor and management. In the case of Taft-Hartley, for example, many employers believe that even sterner measures than Title II are needed to get to the root of emergency strikes, such as a ban on industry-wide bargaining; on the other hand, many

---

[23]Benjamin Aaron, "Public-Interest Disputes and Their Settlement: Observations on the United States Experience," *Labor Law Journal,* vol. 14, no. 8 (August 1963), p. 747.

[24]*ibid.*

[25]See the remarks of James R. Wolfe and Eli L. Oliver in Dallas L. Jones, ed., *Proceedings of the Eighteenth Annual Meeting of the National Academy of Arbitrators, 1965* (Washington: Bureau of National Affairs, 1965), ch. 2, pp. 42–54.

Current Controls on Emergency Strikes

union leaders believe that the emergency issue is an antilabor hoax and would like to see Title II dropped altogether from the law. Caught between these opposing positions, legislators are understandably reluctant to move one way or the other without compelling cause.

Also, the critics' case against these laws is exceedingly difficult to prosecute in one respect. These first three chapters have shown that public opinion apparently favors government intervention in major labor disputes, such intervention has consistently occurred for many years, and the experts themselves insist that few, if any, strikes in these years have actually created emergencies. From this sequence of facts, it is far easier for an elected official to conclude that present strike controls are pretty good than to conclude that they should be scrapped, or that emergencies would still not have happened if the government had done less, or that these controls actually created some of the impasses they were called upon to resolve. The experts may be perfectly right, but it is easy to see why they have convinced other experts more easily than public officials.

Probably the greatest obstacle to change in this policy area, however, is the difficulty critics have in coming up with an alternative proposal that looks much better than the present laws dealing with emergency strikes. Everyone can agree that the model strike control is one which will only be used when really necessary, will always stop every strike to which it is applied, and yet will have no adverse effects on the parties' private bargaining. There is no doubt that the Taft-Hartley and Railway Labor Acts fall miles short of that ideal, but the practical question is whether there is another policy that would come any closer. It is to that question that we now turn.

IV

The Search for a Better Strike Policy

TO ILLUSTRATE THE DIFFICULTIES that have beset both political parties on this issue, it is only necessary to recall a few of the postwar attempts to improve upon existing strike controls.

In the 1952 steel stoppage, President Truman refused to apply the Taft-Hartley procedures, arguing that the union had already postponed its strike for over 80 days at his request and that he believed the employers to be primarily responsible for the impasse. Instead, the President seized the steel mills, the workers promptly returned to their jobs, the companies just as promptly moved to challenge the seizure, and the Supreme Court ruled that the President lacked authority for his action.[1] As a result, the seizure was terminated and the strike was resumed, to last for 55 days in the middle of the Korean War.

In the 1959 steel strike, President Eisenhower also refused at first to apply the Taft-Hartley procedures, but for a very different reason, "I believe that we have got...to test out and to use

---

[1]Youngstown Sheet and Tube Co. v. Sawyer, 343 U. S. 579 (1952).

the method of free bargaining, and the second that we try to bring...bargaining...about by pressure of Government..., then I believe it's not free."[2] On the 35th day of the strike, the Secretary of Labor released a detailed summary of the facts concerning wages, prices, profits, and productivity in the steel industry. He drew no conclusions from these figures, but each of the parties applauded the report as supporting its position, and the strike continued. On its 76th day, the President declared the strike "an intolerable situation" which "must not continue"[3] and called the union and management negotiators to the White House, where he promised government action if a voluntary settlement were not reached soon. After 116 days, the President invoked Taft-Hartley, the strikers returned to work, and a settlement was reached during the period of the injunction.

President Kennedy had the misfortune of inheriting the railroad dispute over the use of diesel firemen and other work rules. In the last months of the Eisenhower administration, the years-long battle over this issue had appeared to be heading into a strike showdown before the then Secretary of Labor, James Mitchell, persuaded the parties to forego the normal emergency board procedures of the Railway Labor Act and instead submit their dispute to a tripartite board, which would have more time and resources for extensive fact-finding and what came to be known as "continuous bargaining." This promising experiment lasted about a year, carrying over into the Kennedy administration, but it failed to produce a peaceful settlement. There then followed, over the course of the next year and a half, the events described in earlier pages: the appointment of a "normal" emergency board, litigation in the courts, mediation by another Secretary of Labor (Willard Wirtz), a proposal by the President that the dispute be arbitrated by a member of the Supreme Court (rejected by the

[2]Transcript of the President's press conference of July 15, 1959 in *New York Times,* July 16, 1959, p. 8.

[3]*New York Times,* Sept. 29, 1959, p. 1.

unions), the appointment by the President of another special committee (including two Cabinet members), strike postponements at the request of the President and then of congressional leaders, extensive hearings before Senate and House committes—and in August 1963, when all these efforts had failed, the first peacetime imposition of compulsory arbitration by the federal government.

In January 1966, President Johnson told Congress, "The recent transit strike in New York City illustrates our helplessness in preventing extreme disruption to the lives and livelihoods of a city of eight million people. I intend to ask the Congress to consider measures that...will enable us to deal effectively with strikes that may cause irreparable damage to the national interest."[4] During the next year and a half, pressure mounted on the Administration to deliver on its pledge: in the summer of 1966, a 43-day airlines strike was exhaustively investigated by Congress and the Senate passed a resolution that would have stopped the strike for up to 180 days; in the fall of 1966, newspapers reported that the President had quietly set up a special study group to report by mid-December on ways to improve existing strike legislation,[5] but no report was ever officially released; when the new 90th Congress assembled in January 1967, a bipartisan group of 14 senators introduced a resolution to require the Secretary of Labor to give Congress his recommendations on this issue;[6] in March, the country's first nationwide lockout occurred in the trucking industry; in April, a major rubber strike began; and in May and June, Congress was reluctantly considering the President's proposal to resolve the railroad shopcraft dispute by compulsory arbitration—and several members of that august body, particularly Republicans, were loudly asking whatever happened to the President's prom-

[4]*Economic Report of the President, January 1966* (Washington: GPO, 1966), p. 17. The President also made the same pledge in his 1966 State of the Union address.

[5]*New York Times,* Nov. 30, 1966, p. 1.

[6]Bureau of National Affairs, *Daily Labor Report,* Jan. 12, 1967, no. 8, p. AA-1.

ise eighteen months earlier to propose new strike legislation. At that point President Johnson deftly tossed the ball back to his critics by inviting Congress to come forward with *its* proposals.[7]

Why did the President fail to offer the recommendations he had promised? Undoubtedly because of one (or all) of the following reasons:

> Some Johnson detractors say he has refused to propose a bill because he wants to avoid antagonizing organized labor. Others believe he cannot face the issue unless there is a crisis, and then the pressure for a law is so great that a broader measure cannot be considered calmly.

> The President's closest advisers say he would like to propose legislation and bury the controversy if he could find something palatable.

> "As soon as we have the right answer, we will send it up," one key aide said. "But it's very difficult to find the right answer."

> "If you talk to eight different guys on this, you get eight different answers," says one ranking official. "Nobody has a solution."[8]

By mid-1968, President Johnson, like his three postwar predecessors, had still not discovered "a solution" to emergency strikes. But also like its own predecessors, neither had the 90th Congress. As a result, the emergency strike provisions of the Taft-Hartley and Railway Labor Acts remained largely unloved and unwanted—and still on the books.

This 20-year record of bipartisan frustration can be better understood by examining the major options available to those who would like to change the existing strike laws.

Proposals to Minimize Government Intervention

As with most issues of public concern, the first and most basic question in this field is whether *any* kind of government control is really needed. The case for free collective bargaining, and against some or all types of strike controls, was presented

---

[7]*New York Times,* June 21, 1967, p. 20.

[8]*New York Times,* April 13, 1967, p. 37.

in Chapter I: the political and economic advantages of permitting private parties to settle their affairs by themselves whenever possible; the necessity of the strike threat to induce voluntary compromise at the bargaining table; the belief that strikes are vastly overrated as to their frequency and their impact upon the public; and the belief that antistrike laws are unable to produce either more peace or more justice in the labor market. To the many adherents of this view, less attention should be paid to tinkering with strike legislation and far more effort should be devoted to improving the procedures that now exist for settling union-management differences on a voluntary basis, namely, private bargaining and government mediation.

Strengthening the Bargaining Process

No one pretends that the private bargaining process is perfect, and a number of its staunchest friends have urged labor and management to recognize that their best defense against government intervention is the voluntary improvement of their negotiating practices. For example, several changes have been suggested to reduce the likelihood that the parties will stumble into a strike that neither party actually wants or needs. The most popular of these proposals is that termed "continuous bargaining," in which the parties tackle particularly complex issues in a study-group setting over an extended period of time and often with the help of neutral experts. This approach contrasts sharply with the more typical deadline bargaining, in which there is often little time or incentive to do more than threaten and bluff. Although continuous bargaining failed on the railroads, it has scored impressively in the steel, meat-packing, and West Coast longshoring industries.

Other proposals aimed at the same target include more meetings of union and management leaders outside of the supercharged atmosphere of negotiating sessions, either to improve mutual understanding in general or to work on specific problems in which the parties have a common interest; more meetings of both parties with neutral experts and public officials, to gain a better understanding of the wider implications of their private bargains; improving grievance handling during the course of a contract, the activity that actually comprises the bulk of union-management dealings and thus can determine the tenor of periodic contract negotiations; making a greater joint effort to gather needed facts from both private and public sources as early as possible in negotiations; and calling upon third parties for private mediation or expert knowledge on the issues in dispute.[9] Most of these proposals have already achieved limited adoption, such as the attempt to improve communication between the parties (in the establishment of the President's Advisory Committee on Labor-Management Policy, the Construction Industry Joint Council at the national level, and annual meetings of construction labor and management in New York State) and the attempt to improve "sick" grievance procedures (for example, in International Harvester and Kaiser Steel and on missile sites).

The defenders of private bargaining nevertheless acknowledge, and indeed stress, that complete industrial harmony is an unrealistic goal in a free society. No matter how skilled and knowledgeable the negotiators, some bargaining impasses will inevitably occur—but, it is argued, this does not mean that crippling strikes are equally inevitable. Three methods have been suggested by which labor and management could voluntarily limit the impact of their disagreements on the public and thereby remove the need for government intervention:

Voluntary arbitration, under which the parties agree not to strike or lockout and to submit their contract dispute to a third party whose decision will be final and binding. The advantage

[9]See, for example, David L. Cole, *The Quest for Industrial Peace* (New York: McGraw-Hill, 1963); W. Willard Wirtz, "The Challenge to Free Collective Bargaining" in *Labor Arbitration and Industrial Change,* Proceedings of the 16th Annual Meeting of the National Academy of Arbitrators (Washington, D. C.: Bureau of National Affairs, 1963), pp. 297–309; and *Free and Responsible Collective Bargaining and Industrial Peace,* Report of the President's Advisory Committee on Labor-Management Policy (Washington. GPO, 1962).

of voluntary, over government-imposed, arbitration is that the parties can decide for themselves such critical matters as who the arbitrators will be, the precise scope of their authority, and the procedures they must follow. Widely used in Great Britain, this technique has been used in this country in parts of the construction industry, some public utilities (particularly urban transit), and to settle the 1968 sanitation strike in New York City.[10] In addition, labor and management leaders in the steel industry actively considered adopting voluntary arbitration as the terminal step in their 1968 negotiations, although the effort eventually failed because of opposition within the union.[11]

Partial operation, meaning that the union and management engaged in a critical shutdown agree to operate enough of the struck facilities to meet the public's most urgent needs. The longshoring, maritime, and airline unions have frequently cooperated with employers in moving defense shipments during their strikes, as did the United Auto Workers with Ford Motor Company during their 1967 strike. The railroad shopcraft unions offered to do the same in their 1967 dispute, and there have been other examples of this approach, such as striking milk drivers continuing deliveries to hospitals.

The non-stoppage strike, a device calling for the parties to continue operation after an impasse is reached, but agreeing to im-

---

[10]For the British experience, see Morrison and Marjorie L. Handsaker, "Arbitration in Great Britain," *Industrial Relations,* vol. 1, no. 1 (October 1961), pp. 117–136. For construction in this country, see "How to Stop Strikes—Before They Start," *Business Week,* Aug. 24, 1963, describing the Council on Industrial Relations which covers "some 95% of the electrical contracting industry" (but not New York City or Chicago); Glenn M. Parker, "The Missile Site Labor Commission," *ILR Research,* vol. 3, no. 1, 1962, pp. 8–15; and Kenneth T. Strand, *Jurisdictional Disputes in Construction: The Causes, the Joint Board, and the NLRB* (Pullman, Washington State University Press, 1961). For public utilities, see Irving Bernstein, *Arbitration of Wages* (Berkeley: University of California Press, 1954), pp. 15–17. For arbitration in the sanitation dispute, see *New York Times,* Feb. 19, 1968, pp. 1 and 44.

[11]*New York Times,* Oct. 27, 1967, p. 29 and the *Wall Street Journal,* Dec. 4, 1967, p. 3.

pose settlement pressures upon themselves in the form of heavy deductions from the workers' pay and the company's income. These sums are to be put into a fund, either to be returned to the parties if they settle within a certain period of time, or given to charity if they fail to meet their self-imposed deadline. Such a plan was tried in 1960 in a Miami bus strike, adopted in 1964 in an Indiana furniture company's labor contract, and proposed but not agreed upon in a 1967 Connecticut dispute.[12]

For our purposes, there is no need for a detailed appraisal of the above proposals for strengthening the private bargaining process. It is clear that the opponents of strike controls have more to offer than slogans deploring the meddlers in Washington or urging negotiators to rise above vulgar self-interest. Instead, they have suggested several specific steps by which labor and management can minimize the need for government intervention and still retain control of their own affairs, and many of these proposals have proved workable in practice.

It is equally clear, of course, that this array of proposals will only evoke from the interventionist his classic counter: if everyone did "the right thing" voluntarily, we certainly would have far fewer social problems on all fronts, including labor relations, but until that miraculous day arrives public policy must cope with the world as it is, not as we wish it to be. In this view, the key point for policy makers today is not that we know several ways to improve private bargaining, but that so few labor-management relationships have adopted these improvements.

Strengthening the Mediation Process

Proposals to improve the mediation process obviously have the same ultimate aim as those above—to help the private

---

[12]The Miami case is described by D. B. McCalmont in "The Semi-Strike," *Industrial and Labor Relations Review*, vol. 15, no. 2 (January 1962), pp. 191–192; the Indiana contract by Neil W. Chamberlain, "Strikes in Contemporary Context," *Industrial and Labor Relations Review*, vol. 20, no. 4 (July 1967), pp. 612–613; and the Connecticut case in the *Wall Street Journal*, March 7, 1967, p. 7.

The Search for a Better Strike Policy

bargaining process perform better—but they differ in that labor and management must assume most of the initiative in carrying out the above proposals, while it is principally the task of government to initiate changes in its own mediation services. In substance, however, the two types of proposals are often very similar.

For example, the most widely hailed innovation on the mediation front in recent years is "preventive mediation," which is described by its chief proponent, the Federal Mediation and Conciliation Service, as follows:

> In carrying out this concept, the Service seeks to provide assistance to labor and management on a year-round, voluntary basis. This assistance is primarily directed toward improving the general labor-management relations climate and eliminating specific problems and irritants that would likely cause serious trouble during contract bargaining or other crisis situations.[13]

More specifically, this approach calls for mediators to encourage the parties to establish joint committees [which "may take the form of prenegotiation committees; postnegotiation committees; study committees (ad hoc); joint. . .committees (continuing); or review and planning committees"]; for mediators also to aid in training foremen and union stewards in grievance handling; to be readily available to consult with the parties on problems arising during the course of a contract; to monitor certain major relationships on a regular basis, and thus provide an "early warning system" to detect impending disputes; and to encourage forums in which labor, management, and public representatives can exchange ideas and become better acquainted.[14]

Clearly, a large part of preventive mediation consists of inducing the private parties to adopt the techniques described earlier for improving the bargaining process. There is, of course, nothing wrong with that, and indeed these worthwhile innovations are undoubtedly spread more effectively by this

---

[13]Federal Mediation and Conciliation Service, *20th Anniversary Report, 1947–1967* (Washington: GPO, 1968), p. 30.

[14]*ibid.*, pp. 32–36.

method, using a staff of skilled mediators in the field, than by any number of speeches by academicians.

Other suggestions for improving mediation include raising the professional status of the staffs of the various mediation agencies, making better use in some cases of special mediators from outside the agencies' staffs, and clarifying the roles of FMCS and the boards of inquiry under Taft-Hartley's emergency provisions.[15]

As mediators themselves are the first to acknowledge, "it is impossible to determine the degree to which mediation has contributed toward a settlement" in any particular dispute,[16] and it is even more difficult to pass judgment on the mediation process as a whole. The arguments on this score are not unlike those over the effectiveness of the United Nations. Everyone can agree that it is better to talk than to fight, and that skilled neutrals can be particularly helpful in disputes between parties who are weak, inexperienced, or in need of a face-saving avenue of retreat. But, ask the skeptics, does peaceful persuasion have much chance of success, on either the domestic or international fronts, in a clash between two of the big powers, each with the strength and experience and determination to take on the other? Or in those cases do we need some way of disarming the disputants before they can inflict too much damage, on themselves and others? Without straining this parallel any further (there is, after all, a world of difference between any strike and any war), it should be clear why nearly everyone favors the idea of improving the mediation process, but why there is far less agreement on how effective this step would be in minimizing the threat of emergency strikes.

One final complication. In its purest form, "free collective bargaining" implies that the private parties control all the power bearing on a particular dispute, and that any mediator

---

[15]Cole, p. 61; and an unofficial report on the recommendations of President Johnson's task force on emergency strike legislation in Bureau of National Affairs, *Daily Labor Report,* Jan. 20, 1967, no. 14, p. A-6.

[16]Federal Mediation and Conciliation Service, *op. cit.,* p. 39.

(whose services the parties are free to reject) can influence negotiations only through his skill and knowledge. In most "major league" disputes, of course, practice falls far short of this ideal. Even when a low-ranking mediator quietly meets with the parties in a major industry, the negotiators are fully aware that the consequences of a failure to agree may be a Taft-Hartley injunction or, on the rails and airlines, an emergency board or possibly even action by Congress. When the President himself publicly "invites" negotiators to Washington and urges them to continue meeting in the shadow of the White House until a settlement is reached, the mediators in these cases—frequently including a member or two of the Cabinet—represent not only the majesty of the Presidential office, but also the political power of the executive branch to initiate administrative or congressional action of direct interest to the parties, not to mention the economic power accruing to the government as the single largest purchaser in the economy.

These comments are meant not to belittle the solid contributions of the mediation process, but simply as a reminder that today the line between "voluntarism" and "government intervention" in collective bargaining can be a very fine one indeed.

Proposals to Make Intervention More Effective

The arguments in favor of strike controls of some kind have already been presented, at least by implication: the belief that in some bargaining relationships, even a brief shutdown can inflict serious harm upon consumers or on other workers and employers; in some other relationships, a brief shutdown would be tolerable in its effects, but the parties have the staying power to prolong a stoppage far beyond that period of tolerance; in cases of doubt concerning the ultimate length and impact of a major strike, the doubt should be resolved in favor of protecting society as a whole, not the interests of the private combatants; the government has in fact intervened in most major strikes, thereby undermining the argument that we have seldom suffered emergencies from strikes in the past and also demonstrating that intervention is not a fatal blight upon collective bargaining; and, finally, a belief that a free society seldom has to choose between total control and no controls whatever, but usually can devise some balance among the competing interests of various groups.

Also, we have described the reasons why some people believe that existing strike controls are quite adequate. In this view, the emergency provisions of both the Taft-Hartley and Railway Labor Acts provide a moderate compromise among the rights of those affected by a critical strike. Both laws arm the President with a means of stopping such a strike for a cooling-off period of 60 to 80 days, but neither authorizes the government to impose a settlement upon the parties. The record shows that the parties have nearly always complied with these temporary strike bans and have often reached peaceful settlements either during or after the cooling-off period. On the other hand, if these measures do not produce a voluntary settlement, the private parties are legally free to resume a stoppage and the federal authorities still have several options, from doing nothing to passing a compulsory arbitration law to apply only to the dispute in question.

For reasons such as these, a recent report by the National Association of Manufacturers concluded that Taft-Hartley's emergency strike procedure "has preserved collective bargaining with only a needed minimum of federal interposition, and represents a workable melding of the country's basic labor-management needs with the preservation of a free economy."[17] The report therefore recommended that this section of Taft-Hartley, *"having worked well, should be left as it is."*[18]

---

[17]National Association of Manufacturers, "Big Labor and Big Strikes: Analysis and Recommendations," Report of Subcommittee on Emergency Disputes of NAM Industrial Relations Committee in Bureau of National Affairs, *Daily Labor Report,* Sept. 18, 1967, no. 181, p. D-4.

[18]*ibid.* Italics in original text.

The Search for a Better Strike Policy

On the other side of the fence, some labor leaders have also had some second thoughts. On the occasion of the twentieth anniversary of Taft-Hartley, A. H. Raskin wrote:

> The Taft-Hartley Act, denounced by unions as a "slave labor law" when it went into effect twenty years ago ..., now has more vehement critics in industry than it does in unions.
>
> . . . .
>
> The provision of the law that worried labor most—empowering the President to get an eighty-day injunction to halt a strike he considers dangerous to the national health or safety—has now become a union shield against Congressional moves for compulsory arbitration to end strike emergencies.
>
> Every proposal for more dependable public safeguards against crippling tie-ups in key industries brings from labor the argument that the Taft-Hartley machinery has prevented any dispute from reaching a crisis stage so acute that the country was subjected to intolerable hardship.
>
> Oddly, there is increasing popularity among some union legal experts for a project to substitute the national emergency provision of the Taft law for the strike restraints in the Railway Labor Act, a law put on the books in 1926 with the blessings of the railroad unions.[19]

Too much should not be read into this apparent burst of labor-management harmony over strike controls, however. The implication is clear in the above that labor leaders still do not think Taft-Hartley's strike controls are fair or necessary, but only less deplorable than the possible alternative of compulsory arbitration. For its part, the NAM coupled its praise of Taft-Hartley with a plea that Congress address itself to the "root cause of the whole problem," namely, "the aggregation of union power" that permits a normal labor dispute to be "escalated at the whim of a vast union enterprise into a crisis of national dimensions."[20] And neither labor nor management quite knows what to do with the Railway Labor Act.

The search therefore continues for a better strike policy,

---

[19]"That 'Slave Labor Law' Twenty Years Later" in *New York Times*, Aug. 21, 1967, p. 30.

[20]National Association of Manufacturers, *op. cit.*, pp. D-1, 3.

with the "interventionists" favoring one or more of the following proposals: seizure, compulsory arbitration, the statutory strike, or the arsenal-of-weapons approach.

Seizure

In his recent and definitive study, *Presidential Seizure in Labor Disputes,* John L. Blackman, Jr. explodes several widely held notions about the seizure weapon, such as the beliefs that it has seldom been used, is patently unconstitutional, and is always either too weak or too powerful (both views are held) in its effects on the parties. Blackman discovered that there have been 71 seizures in labor disputes during our history, the first in 1864 and the last in 1952. Sixty of these actions were taken under various laws expressly authorizing coercion in emergency disputes, and the courts always upheld these actions whenever they were challenged; of the other 11 seizures, in which the President acted without express statutory authorization, only one was challenged in the courts, but in that one—the 1952 steel case—the President's action was overturned.[21]

As for the belief that seizure involves little more than running the flag up over a plant and is therefore a paper tiger, Blackman found that the government has exerted a wide variety of pressures on whichever party offered resistance. Injunctions have been obtained against strikes in the face of a seizure; company officials as well as union members have frequently been discharged and replaced for the duration of a seizure; government officials have sometimes taken control of all the major operational decisions, from hiring and firing to sales and production methods; and workers' wages and working conditions have been either changed or not changed during the seizure period, depending on which party was resisting the government take-over. As for the opposing belief that seizure is such a potent weapon that it overwhelms the private parties and becomes compulsory arbitration in effect if not in

[21]John L. Blackman, Jr., *Presidential Seizure in Labor Disputes* (Cambridge, Mass.: Harvard University Press, 1967), ch. 1.

The Search for a Better Strike Policy

name, Blackman again found the facts to be less tidy than the myth. In 20 percent of the cases, either one or both of the private parties defied the seizure action—by strikes, protests to Congress, and other means—to the point at which the presidents either abandoned the seizures or yielded concessions in order to achieve partial control.[22]

The historical record thus suggests that the courts would uphold a statute authorizing seizure in emergency disputes, although past decisions to this effect were doubtless influenced by the fact that all the seizures challenged took place just before, during, or shortly after a war (as, in fact, did all 71 seizures). The record also indicates that this weapon, like all other strike controls, cannot offer an absolute guarantee that it will always stop a critical strike, much less produce a settlement satisfactory to all concerned.

Of particular interest, however, is Blackman's demonstration that seizure can mean very different things in different situations. At one extreme, it can mean that the government takes over a company only on paper, leaving the management free to run the business as usual and retain all profits earned, while the government concentrates on trying to smash any strike by securing injunctions, firing strikers, using military personnel as replacements, and other similar methods. Even if the workers promptly and peacefully return to work at the moment of seizure, this type of intervention clearly remains one-sided, for it strips the union of its strike power and fails to substitute any other economic pressure on management to yield anything in negotiations. At the other extreme, seizure can mean that the government replaces top management, makes all the operating decisions, impounds profits, and institutes the changes in wages and working conditions that management refused to accept in bargaining. In this case, the employer's derision is justified when he is told that the seizure will continue until he reaches an agreement with the union, but of course he is free to

---

[22]*ibid.*, chs. 2–4.

93

negotiate for something less than the government has already granted the union "for the interim"!

Thus, in appraising seizure as a strike control, one must first ask: "Which kind of seizure?" One of the most sophisticated variations has been proposed by Senator Jacob K. Javits, who for several years has championed seizure as an improvement upon existing strike controls. His most recent bill to this effect provides the following procedure:

1. Taft-Hartley's emergency provisions would be altered to give the President a choice between using the present procedure or a procedure modeled on the Railway Labor Act. Under the latter, the President could direct the board of inquiry to make recommendations and could also direct the parties not to engage in a stoppage for up to 30 days after the board reports. The injunction and last-offer ballot would be dropped under this alternative. The Railway Labor Act's emergency provisions would remain unchanged up to this point.

2. Both the Taft-Hartley and Railway Labor Acts would be amended to permit their application not only to nationwide disputes but also to those that "imperil the health or safety of a substantial part of the population." Taft-Hartley also could be applied to disputes in "transportation, transmission, or communication" industries affecting commerce, even when the employer is a State or local government. These changes are designed to cover local disputes such as those in the New York City transit system.

3. If the above procedures failed to resolve an emergency dispute, both acts would permit the President (through the Attorney General) to petition a federal district court "for the appointment of a special receiver to take immediate possession in the name of the United States of any plant, mine, or facility which is the subject of such labor dispute and to use and operate such...facility in the interests of the United States."

4. If the court approves a seizure petition, wages and other employment conditions shall either be frozen *or* the court may direct the receiver to institute *some or all* of any changes recommended by the Presidential board in step 1. Note that this authority rests with the court and not the President, and that it is entirely discretionary.

5. The employer may choose either to have the facility operated for his account—that is, he would receive any profits made or suffer any loss incurred during seizure—or he may waive all such claims

and elect to have the federal government pay him "just, fair, and reasonable compensation" for the use of his property. If he chooses the latter course, he will not necessarily receive a sum equal to full rental value or some equivalent standard, for the government is authorized to deduct something for the fact that the facility might have been closed by a strike if it had not been seized. If the employer disagrees with the government's offer, he may appeal the decision in the courts.

6. During the seizure, the parties "shall be encouraged" to continue bargaining. The special receiver is forbidden to negotiate a contract with the union. The facility shall be returned to the employer no later than 30 days after an agreement is negotiated or the emergency threat is removed in some other way.

7. At all points in this procedure, both acts would strongly promote partial operation. Before permitting seizure, a district court could "direct the parties to the dispute to make every effort to agree to continue or resume such part of the operations...as in the opinion of the court is necessary to protect the health or safety of the Nation or any substantial part of the population or territory thereof." If the parties cannot reach such an agreement voluntarily, the court still must restrict the special receiver to operate the facility only to the extent necessary to protect health or safety.[23]

This carefully drawn bill illustrates both the flexibility and the hazards of seizure as a strike control. Its chances of stopping a strike are at least as favorable as those of the present injunction under Taft-Hartley or the waiting period under the Railway Labor Act, without their disadvantage of expiring after 60 or 80 days whether the emergency has been averted or not. By the same token, this proposal offers as much "finality" as compulsory arbitration, but without the necessity for the government to dictate the terms of settlement. In addition, several provisions of the bill obviously introduce the element of uncertainty stressed by the arsenal-of-weapons approach (described below), some introduce the pressure on both parties sought by the statutory strike (also described below), and partial operation is explicitly encouraged.

A basic dilemma in this field, however, is that any law which

---

[23]Bill S.1456 in the 90th Congress, as reproduced in Bureau of National Affairs, *Daily Labor Report*, April 7, 1967, no. 68, pp. D-1, 2.

narrowly limits the discretion of those administering it, such as Taft-Hartley, is criticized for being too rigid and predictable —while any proposal that permits a great deal of discretion to its administrators, such as the Javits' bill, will be criticized for its vulnerability to abuse. For example, when a receiver is instructed under this bill to operate a company "in the interests of the United States," does this mean he will not take over any decision making so long as management continues to get out the production or does it mean something more? What standards should the court use in deciding the extent of partial operation necessary? Or in deciding whether none, some, or all of a board's recommendations on wages and employment conditions should be instituted for the duration of the seizure? If the court simply orders a freeze of existing wages and conditions, and management elects to take its normal profits, what pressure would this bill exert on the employer to compromise? Is a federal judge the best choice to make these difficult judgments, designed to nudge a union and management toward a voluntary agreement? But if a President of either party were granted this discretionary authority, would he inspire any more confidence than a judge?

In short, seizure has far more flexibility as a strike control than is commonly realized, but it shares several problems with the other controls we shall now consider.

Compulsory Arbitration

The case against compulsory arbitration was presented in Chapter I: the belief that it "not only would wipe out strikes but it would wipe out collective bargaining,"[24] because neither party, and particularly the weaker one, would have an incentive to compromise on anything; settlements imposed by neutrals will not necessarily be any more equitable, and will usually be far less acceptable, than a solution worked out by

---

[24]The comment of an unidentified "observer" of President Johnson's task force on emergency strikes, as reported in Bureau of National Affairs, *Daily Labor Report*, Jan. 20, 1967, no. 14, p. A-6.

the parties themselves; wage fixing will probably lead to price fixing; and there is no assurance that this weapon will stop an emergency strike.

These points are naturally challenged by the very small handful of experts who favor some form of compulsory arbitration. On the philosophical level, one has argued:

> Over the years, the case against compulsory arbitration of labor disputes has been argued with such skill and conviction that the brief for the defense seems to have been lost. Quite apart from the merits, this is a curious development in a community where the compulsory arbitration of other types of dispute is considered an ornament of a free society. If a neighbor commits a trespass or a business associate fails to honor his contract, he is hailed before a magistrate and the matter is compulsorily arbitrated rather than settled by force of arms. Even in the difficult and delicate areas of domestic relations, questions of child custody and separate maintenance may be brought to compulsory arbitration at the option of an aggrieved party. Our whole system of jurisprudence relies on the idea that anyone with a grievance is able to compel an antagonist to meet him peaceably at a public hearing where, after argument, a binding third-party settlement is handed down. No one apologizes for this; more often than not the courts are referred to as protectors of our liberties, defenders of freedom.[25]

The same author, Orme Phelps, also stresses that third-party settlement already has virtually eliminated the strike in two of the three principal categories of labor disputes. First, disputes over whether management should recognize a union as spokesman for its workers—the recognition issue that led to some of the bloodiest strikes in our history—are now settled primarily by the "compulsory arbitration" of agencies such as the National or New York State Labor Relations Boards. Second, of the many thousands of grievances that arise across the country every day in the application of labor-management agreements, the vast majority are subject to no-strike clauses and, in the absence of voluntary settlement by the parties, to binding decision by a neutral. The third category of disputes,

---

[25]Orme W. Phelps, "Compulsory Arbitration: Some Perspectives," *Industrial and Labor Relations Review,* vol. 18, no. 1 (October 1964), p. 81.

those over the terms of a new contract, may or may not be amenable to the same process, but Phelps argues that at least this question should not be decided by the stock notion that it is faintly un-American to settle a labor dispute by impartial decree rather than on a picket line. On the contrary, he estimates that "probably as many issues go to compulsory arbitration in the United States each year as are settled by the parties on their own."[26]

But what of the key charge that, if compulsory arbitration were extended to this third category of contract disputes, bargaining would be destroyed because one or both parties would be tempted to push everything to arbitration? Most critics of this weapon argue that it is dangerous to generalize from third-party settlement of grievances and law cases, for the arbiters in those disputes are primarily interpreting an existing contract clause or statute, not writing new law in the sense of deciding the size of a general wage increase or whether there should be a compulsory membership clause. Phelps nevertheless considers it significant that most grievances and NLRB cases are settled before reaching the point at which a third-party decision is necessary, and he doubts that contract disputes are actually so different that the parties will settle few by themselves. Also, he reminds the critics that any peacetime compulsory arbitration law would undoubtedly apply only to critical industries or disputes, so that the entire institution of collective bargaining is hardly at stake in this debate, as is sometimes implied.[27] Finally, if labor and management truly find the idea of compulsory arbitration so repugnant, that in itself might spur them to bargain in good faith in order to head off this form of intervention.

There are more specific ways, however, of inducing the

---

[26]*ibid.*, p. 83. Most authorities classify grievance arbitration as voluntary rather than compulsory arbitration, but Phelps argues, "The contractual undertaking to submit unresolved issues to arbitration is voluntary but, once incorporated in an agreement, is compulsory and legally enforceable," *ibid.*, p. 84.

[27]*ibid.*, pp. 85–90.

parties to bargain genuinely when arbitration replaces the strike as the final equalizer. For example, Carl Stevens has described an ingenious proposal to require the arbitrator to adopt as his award *the final prearbitration position of one party or the other*.[28] By thus removing the parties' expectation that the arbitrator will split the difference in their prearbitration positions, this proposal would penalize the clinging to extreme demands and would provide a powerful inducement to both parties either to reach a voluntary agreement or, at the very least, to narrow their differences toward the point of honest disagreement which they might have reached at a strike deadline.

Yet another proposal, this by Neil Chamberlain, rests on the premise, "Since the problem of compulsory arbitration arises from the fact that it is virtually costless, the evident solution is to make compulsory arbitration costly."[29] Members of government boards are nearly always paid from public funds, and even privately appointed arbitrators seldom cost the parties more than $200 or $300 a day. This proposal is to make any compulsory arbitration board's services about as expensive to the parties as a strike would be.

> The cost might range from perhaps $25,000 to $100,000 a day for each party. The same charge could be made to each party, ... or a sliding scale could be introduced which would base the union's cost on the number of members involved in the strike and the company's cost on its assets, with some maximum in both cases. If a major strike in steel...should be judged to affect adversely the public's interests, for example, ... the cost of the board's services might be set at the maximum limit (say $100,000 a day), so that a thirty-day arbitration proceeding would cost each party $3 million.[30]

The rebuttals to the other criticisms of compulsory arbitration may be described more briefly. To the charge that

[28]Carl M. Stevens, "Is Compulsory Arbitration Compatible with Bargaining?" *Industrial Relations*, vol. 5, no. 2 (February 1966), pp. 45–47.

[29]Neil W. Chamberlain, *The Labor Sector* (New York: McGraw-Hill, 1965), p. 643.

[30]*ibid.*

arbitrators have no firm guidelines by which to decide contract issues "correctly," the response is that this is true but neither have the parties, and an experienced neutral can usually spot several clues to a "reasonable" settlement (such as the terms of other current settlements). Indeed, if this were not true, what would be the purpose of the frequent proposal that Taft-Hartley boards be given the right to make recommendations? To the allied charge that arbitration awards will be less acceptable to the parties than voluntary agreements, several answers are made: this may be true, but it is a necessary price to pay to avert a critical stoppage; the parties have learned to live with settlements imposed by grievance arbitrators and agencies such as the NLRB; and the awards can be made more acceptable by permitting labor and management to select the third party, define the issues to be decided, and participate in a tripartite board making the final award.

As for the argument that compulsory arbitration cannot guarantee a cessation of emergency strikes, the obvious retort is that neither can any other strike control yet devised, which simply returns one to the basic question of whether any kind of strike control should be adopted. If your answer is yes, then compulsory arbitration probably has as good a chance of being obeyed (or defied) as most other controls; if your answer is no, then the issue of compliance is academic anyway. Finally, the prediction that wage control must lead to price control does not seem to have been explicitly considered by the recent defenders of compulsory arbitration, but presumably they would answer in one of two ways: either that there are few peacetime precedents for assuming that intervention in the labor market must be mirrored in the product market, or that there is indeed a need for selective arbitration of key price, as well as wage, decisions in order to cope with the inflationary pressures of a full-employment economy. (We return to this last issue in the last chapter.)

That, in brief, is the case for compulsory arbitration. It cannot be dismissed as the rantings of those who detest all strikes and most unions. On the contrary, the basic appeal of compulsory arbitration has always been one of equity: if society believes that it cannot tolerate a particular strike, then it owes the parties involved—and especially labor—the right to have their dispute promptly settled by some other method that is fair to both.

Thus, compulsory arbitration is not only the most "extreme" of the proposed alternatives to the strike, but in one sense is also the most "honest." Other controls, such as seizure and the injunction, rest on a hope that collective bargaining can somehow function even without labor's right to strike. The critics of strike controls challenge this contention, asserting that you can settle a labor dispute by either free collective bargaining or government control, but you cannot have a little of both. Compulsory arbitration squarely faces up to this choice that few people (in either camp) care to make.

Or does it? If this distasteful choice must indeed be made, why does Phelps argue so strongly that the adoption of compulsory arbitration will not really displace all voluntary decision making, or why do other advocates devise variations to prod the parties into genuine bargaining, such as Chamberlain's proposal to make arbitration as costly as the strike? The answer, of course, is that even the "interventionists" in a free society certainly *prefer* voluntary agreement to government dictation and wish to give the former every possible chance to do the job.

This also must explain in part the refusal of Congress so far to adopt any of the bills before it that provide for compulsory arbitration in all emergency disputes,[31] and its great reluctance to adopt those arbitration measures which applied only to the 1963 and 1967 rail disputes. Why else should Congress oppose a strike control that wins much public support in opinion polls and, in recent years, has also been endorsed by many

---

[31]See, for example, Senator George A. Smathers' bill to create a court of labor-management relations, described in Bureau of National Affairs, *Daily Labor Report*, Oct. 18, 1967, no. 203, pp. A-10–A-12.

employers in the railroad and maritime industries, two of the leading targets of any such proposal? One reason for this opposition is certainly the political power of organized labor, which has gone down the line against compulsory arbitration in private industry, but surely another reason is that many legislators sincerely share the repugnance felt by labor leaders (and employers) toward the idea of fixing wages and working conditions by public edict instead of private negotiation.

It is probably true that compulsory arbitration does not differ as radically from other strike controls as it first appears. The other controls are not unique in their attempt to preserve some inducement for voluntary agreement, as shown by Phelps's persuasive arguments that much private bargaining would still take place under compulsory arbitration, and the promising innovations in the arbitration process suggested by Chamberlain and Stevens for just this purpose. Nor does compulsory arbitration have a monopoly on coercion, for we have seen that if labor or management defies a seizure action, for example, the federal authorities can and have wheeled up highly coercive weapons of enforcement.

Yet, the fact remains that no other strike control so *openly and directly* threatens to impose a final decision on the parties if they cannot settle a critical dispute by themselves. For that reason, if no other, the search will continue for a strike policy with a more palatable blend of coercion and voluntarism than that offered by compulsory arbitration.

The Statutory Strike

Earlier in this chapter, the "non-stoppage strike" was described as one of the methods by which labor and management could voluntarily limit the impact of their disagreements on the public. Some people have proposed that this method of settlement—also called the semi-strike and the statutory strike —be enacted into law so that the government could require its use in an emergency dispute.

The essence of this proposal is to require forfeits by labor

The Search for a Better Strike Policy

and management as a substitute for the strike. There is disagreement over just how this should be done, but the following summary of one plan will indicate the general drift of most:

1. The President may seek an injunction to stop a critical strike for a period of up to 140 days.

2. Each worker in the bargaining unit then chooses whether to "strike" by agreeing (or not agreeing) that his gross earnings will be reduced by a certain percentage. *The employer must match each worker's deduction, dollar for dollar, and forward both parties' forfeits to the public treasury as a "strike tax."*

3. The deduction rate might be at any level between 10 and 100 percent, with the exact proportion to be determined by the President on a case-by-case basis. A reasonable norm might be 40 percent, but the rate could be higher if stalemates were occurring too frequently or lower in an industry in which wages form a high proportion of total costs (and the "normal" rate might therefore place an impossible burden on employers).

4. As a further inducement to settle, the strike deadline is repeatedly simulated by requiring that strike taxes are payable every seventh day of the injunction period. If the parties settle their dispute during the first seven-day subperiod, their strike taxes for that week are refunded (or not collected). If they do not settle by the seventh day, their taxes for that first week are collected and permanently lost. This process is repeated weekly until a settlement is reached or the injunction expires after twenty weeks and twenty such deadlines.

5. It would be an unfair labor practice for an employer to replace or otherwise discriminate against a "striker," but workers could still be disciplined as usual for unsatisfactory work performance.[32]

This plan obviously attempts to combine the strengths and

---

[32]Stephen H. Sosnick, "Non-Stoppage Strikes: A New Approach," *Industrial and Labor Relations Review*, vol. 18, no. 1 (October 1964), pp. 73–80. This article also surveys the literature on this type of strike control.

minimize the weaknesses of the other major approaches to the strike problem. Unlike the free-collective-bargaining approach, the statutory strike aims to maintain output while the parties fight out their differences. Unlike the injunction or the "paper seizure," this plan puts some heat on management as well as on labor. Unlike fact-finding or compulsory arbitration, this plan requires no outsider to suggest or decide what the settlement terms should be. In short, this proposal would retain most of the voluntary and power aspects of the bargaining process at a minimum cost in government intervention and lost production —if it worked.

But will it work? Ideally, the forfeits under this plan should either put equal pressure on labor and management or should duplicate the same unequal pressures that an actual strike would produce in a particular relationship. The sad truth, however, is that no one knows how to measure these concepts of pressure and power in a specific union-management relationship.

Indeed, a major cause of strikes is that the participants themselves disagree about their relative strengths. How, then, can any law or any President duplicate the relative power of, for example, the United Steelworkers and the steel companies in a strike to the finish, when even the parties know this only after the strike is over (if then)? Even if the more realistic aim of a statutory strike law were to apply *equal* pressure to the parties, rather than to duplicate actual strike pressures, the problems are just as formidable. Using the same example, for every dollar the government "taxes" a steel worker or his union's treasury, how many dollars should it remove from the steel companies in order to place equal pressure on labor and management? Again, no one knows.

This would be a fatal defect of the statutory strike, its defenders argree, if there were some better strike policy available. They point out, however, that *every other strike control yet proposed can also alter the power relationship of the private parties.* We have seen, for instance, that the injunction can strip a union of its primary source of power and thus increase management's strength; a seizure, depending on how it is applied, can render impotent either or both parties; and third parties under compulsory arbitration can either try to duplicate what a voluntary settlement would have yielded, which requires making a string of assumptions about the parties' relative strength, or they can (deliberately or accidentally) award more to one party and less to the other than power alone would have dictated.

In short, runs this argument, the great virtue of the statutory strike is that it spotlights the basic problem facing every strike control—how to bring pressure on both parties to settle without a strike—and forces the government at least to try to be even-handed in applying this pressure. There is admittedly no perfect way of doing this, but other controls give even worse solutions by pretending, in effect, that the problem does not exist.

Two other criticisms of the statutory strike deserve mention, the first being the inevitable question of enforceability. At the level of formal compliance or defiance by labor unions and corporations, this problem would probably be no more (or less) serious for this type of strike control than for any other. But will the individual worker put out his usual effort when his paycheck is cut for any reason by 40 or 50 percent? It is true that management could still discipline workers for excessive absenteeism or slack performance or outright sabotage, and perhaps the public is ahead of the game so long as output continues at any level much above the zero output of a real strike. Anything approaching a mass slowdown is nevertheless very difficult to handle by conventional disciplinary methods and can also increase management's operating costs substantially. Finally, some have also argued that the statutory strike does not offer the same psychological release as a real walkout, but this, of course, is true of all strike controls.

The heart of the controversy over this proposal, however, is its attempt to define the pressure to be put on the parties to an emergency dispute. For the reasons described above, the advocates of the statutory strike believe that even an imperfect formula for equalizing bargaining pressures would be more equitable and effective in inducing voluntary agreement than the process followed under other strike controls, which alter the parties' power relationship without any guides whatever for maintaining a rough equity. But, to its critics, this proposal is wildly unrealistic in its assumption that the essence of a bargaining relationship can be remotely approximated by any forfeiture formula likely to be adopted. Stated differently, it is possible to devise a formula to equalize bargaining pressures, but only in such abstract and complex terms that the formula would not be politically acceptable or administratively feasible. On the other hand, argue the critics, a formula easy to understand and administer—such as the proposal to require management to match each worker's strike tax—will be too arbitrary and inaccurate to win (or deserve) the approval of Congress or the bargaining parties.

V

The Search for a Better
Strike Policy
(Continued)

IT SHOULD NOW BE CLEAR WHY
"probably the most frequently advocated method"[1] of handling
emergency strikes is the arsenal-of-weapons approach, under
which the President would have the authority in each dispute
to choose from among several different strike controls. We
have seen that each and every type of control is attacked on
one ground or another: for giving the President too much
power or not enough, for being too vague or too precise, for
favoring one party or the other. How better to make a virtue
out of necessity than by abandoning the fruitless search for a
single weapon that the parties will find equitable and, instead,
threatening them with most of the weapons they find in-
equitable? Faced with this invitation to play Russian roulette

---

[1]Neil W. Chamberlain, "Strikes in Contemporary Context," *Industrial
and Labor Relations Review,* vol. 20, no. 4 (July 1967), p. 610. For
an excellent appraisal of the only major law incorporating this approach,
see George P. Shultz, "The Massachusetts Choice-of-Procedures Approach
to Emergency Disputes," *Industrial and Labor Relations Review,* vol. 10,
no. 3 (April 1957), pp. 359–374.

with the man in the White House, the parties may well elect to settle their dispute without a strike.

The Arsenal-of-Weapons Approach

Although seldom stated quite so inelegantly, that is the primary argument for the arsenal-of-weapons approach. To be more specific, we know there are good reasons why labor dislikes the injunction, management is hostile to seizure, and both usually loathe compulsory arbitration. Instead of endlessly debating which of these is the least offensive, runs this argument, Congress can capitalize on the fact that they are *all* offensive to one party or the other. Give the President the power to dangle all of these (or other) weapons over the heads of the parties, with no indication of which one he will select in any particular dispute, and the negotiators on both sides of the table will think twice before precipitating a major work stoppage. If a strike nevertheless does occur, the President can trigger any one of the controls available to him and the public will be no worse off than under a single-weapon approach.

A second argument in favor is "the belief that no single procedure is suited to all strike situations."[2] Partial operation may be feasible in some industries but not in others, for example, or public hearings and recommendations may be needed in one negotiation and completely private mediation in another.

The popularity of this proposal is therefore understandable, for while the interventionists cannot agree among themselves on any single-weapon approach, they can all agree on the premises underlying this plan: most of the single weapons have serious flaws; any intervention should preserve or induce as much genuine bargaining as possible; and yet the public should be protected in the event that bargaining results in a critical stoppage. By thus creating strength out of weakness, the arsenal-of-weapons approach demonstrates that the whole may indeed be greater than the sum of its parts.

---

[2]*ibid.*

The Search for a Better Strike Policy

It should surprise no one, however, to learn that it also has its share of critics. To those who believe either that all intervention is deplorable or that some controls are decidedly better than others, there is little merit in authorizing the use of several bad controls. In fact, the advocates of this proposal themselves appear divided on this point. For example, a 1962 statement by President Kennedy's Advisory Committee on Labor-Management Policy is often characterized as advocating an arsenal of weapons, and yet its recommendations were clearly aimed at making Taft-Hartley's strike procedure *more* palatable to the parties, not less. Thus, the committee proposed dropping the injunction and last-offer ballot provisions and adopting in essence the Railway Labor Act's emergency board procedure, but also giving the President a choice of appointing a special mediation board at an early or late stage of critical negotiations and of directing that board either to make or not to make recommendations to the parties and the public.[3]

Compare those mild recommendations with a recent congressional bill that would amend the Railway Labor Act to give the President the following options: to go directly to compulsory arbitration or to appoint an emergency board as now provided in the act; if he chooses the latter route and it fails to settle the dispute, the President could send the board's report to Congress together with his recommendations for further action, or he could issue an Executive Order putting the board's recommendations into effect for 120 days, or he could order compulsory arbitration.[4]

Which of these proposals better represents the arsenal-of-weapons approach? The first obviously stresses the argument that different weapons are needed in different disputes; the second leans more on the argument that the parties should be

---

[3]*Free and Responsible Collective Bargaining and Industrial Peace,* Report of the President's Advisory Committee on Labor-Management Policy (Washington: GPO, 1962), pp. 4–6.

[4]H.R. 5638, introduced in the 90th Congress by Congressman Pickle, as reported in Bureau of National Affairs, *Daily Labor Report,* Feb. 16, 1967, no. 33, p. AA-1.

uncertain as to which of several unpleasant fates await them if they fail to reach a peaceful settlement. Each argument is plausible, but together they pose a dilemma. If a strike law is to stimulate maximum apprehension and uncertainty in the hearts of negotiators, it probably must contain a range of good, bad, and indifferent controls—but if the law aims only to give the President some flexibility in using the few weapons considered good or safe or least offensive, such as mediation and cooling-off periods, then the parties have little to fear from the President's choice.

Nor do the attacks stop there. As previously indicated, some critics argue that existing strike controls already provide most of the flexibility and uncertainty sought by the arsenal-of-weapons approach. The opening section of Chapter IV, for instance, illustrates the fact that every postwar President has felt free to use a variety of settlement techniques in addition to those provided him by the Taft-Hartley and Railway Labor Acts. And for anyone desirous of uncertainty, what could be better than the ultimate weapon now available to the President, namely, tossing an unresolved dispute to the tender mercies of Congress?

Finally, some question the validity of the uncertainty thesis itself. The most worrisome doubt for many negotiators can be the basic one of whether the government will intervene at all in the event of a strike—not the particular form that intervention might take. Or as one group of critics has put this point even more strongly: "What the parties to collective bargaining need is not more uncertainty but more certainty—specifically more certainty that the government will not intervene except in rare emergencies."[5] Whichever version of this point one may prefer, it could be achieved as well under existing law as under an arsenal-of-weapons law. On the other hand, if the hope really is to bluff the parties on the President's choice of weapons, consider the observation of one expert that

---

[5]Committee for Economic Development, *Union Powers and Functions: Toward a Better Balance* (New York, 1964), p. 28.

"any labor or management leader who could not find out what the President was going to do in a given emergency probably was not operating in the big-strike leagues"![6]

In spite of this catalogue of criticisms, the arsenal-of-weapons approach remains popular with many experts. Part of its attraction may well be that, even more than the other proposals we have examined, this plan can mean different things to different people. In its "purest" form, it can appeal to those who have given up any hope of discovering a good single-weapon approach and feel that it is worth trying the other extreme of brandishing all the clumsy weapons available in the hope that none will have to be used. In its more genteel guise, this approach can also claim those who simply want Congress to endorse and encourage all the mediation techniques that the President may now use only on his own initiative.

But the popularity of this approach, however defined, is also a telling commentary on the state of the strike-control art. After more than twenty years of congressional debate, presidential experimentation, and academic research in this field, many believe that the best we can do is trust to executive discretion. It is a pretty question whether this represents a sophisticated awareness that labor disputes are too complex to yield to simple answers and rigid laws—or whether this is one more illustration of how presidential power can expand in direct ratio to the failure of private citizens and Congress to settle their problems for themselves.

Other Proposals

There is yet a third group of proposed strike policies which do not fit neatly into either the category of minimizing government intervention or that of making intervention more effective. The common element in these proposals is the use

---

[6]An unidentified participant in a meeting of experts called in 1961 by Secretary of Labor Arthur Goldberg to advise him on the emergency strike issue. *New York Times*, Aug. 21, 1961, p. 12.

of one type of government intervention in order to avoid having to use another, more distasteful type.

Decentralize the Bargaining Structure

Easily the most popular examples of this approach are the several proposals to apply the antitrust laws to labor unions, to ban industry-wide bargaining, or in other ways to narrow the size of bargaining units. If this were done, it has long been argued by many employers and economists, then free collective bargaining could really work for the first time. Labor and management, that is, would be free to put their disagreements to the ultimate test of a strike, but because no strike could shut down most or all of a critical industry there would be no need for the government to intervene in either the strike or the bargaining process.

Unfortunately, this kind of proposal raises so many complex issues that it can only be given cursory treatment here. As George Hildebrand has shown, there are several varieties and objectives of the proposals to apply the antitrust laws to labor:

> Some of these [proposals] hardly go beyond incantation, and amount to little more than an indiscriminate attack on a whole range of admittedly difficult problems—corruption, coercion, big unionism, national strikes, and even collective bargaining itself. What this line of thinking involves is far more than a return to antitrust. In reality, it intends a complete reconstruction of national labor policy....
>
> The more carefully framed proposals... would renew antitrust to cope with four major problems: national emergency strikes, make-work policies, direct efforts to control the product market, and the effects of collective bargaining upon wages.[7]

On the level of incantation, for example, there is the argument that applying the antitrust laws to labor and management alike is only fair because what is sauce for the goose is sauce for the gander—which has brought the rejoinder that if this

---

[7]George H. Hildebrand, "Collective Bargaining and the Antitrust Laws" in J. Shister, B. Aaron, and C. W. Summers, eds., *Public Policy and Collective Bargaining* (New York: Harper and Row, 1962), p. 171.

means there is no difference between the two, it will be news to a great many geese and ganders. And that, in fact, is the heart of the problem: unions *are* decidedly different from companies, for every union is clearly a "combination to eliminate competition among workingmen in dealing with their employers."[8]

There is nothing sinister or concealed about this need for unions to exercise "monopoly power" to be effective. After all, why would we permit any union to exist if we believed that competition among workers could meet all their legitimate needs? It is therefore no answer to any labor problem to propose the elimination of union monopoly power, unless the aim is to eliminate unions themselves as anything but debating societies. More specifically, if unions were subjected with no qualification to the Sherman Antitrust Act—which outlaws "every contract, combination . . . or conspiracy in restraint of trade or commerce"—this could cast in doubt the legality of every union-management contract and every strike that remotely affects interstate commerce.

This does not mean, however, that society can only choose between exterminating unions and permitting them all the monopoly power they can get. When Congress was formulating the Taft-Hartley Act in 1947, for instance, the Hartley bill originally passed by the House contained a provision outlawing "monopolistic strikes" without outlawing unions themselves:

> In effect, this provision would forbid a strike by a union against more than one employer if the strike action could be identified as resulting from any conspiracy, collusion, or concerted plan of action between employees of competing employers unless the employees had a common bargaining agent. Another provision of the bill...would permit employees of competing employers to have a common bargaining agent only if (1) the bargaining agent represented less than one hundred employees of each employer and (2) the plants of the competing employers were less than fifty miles apart.

[8]*ibid.*, p. 152.

National Emergency Strikes

> What these provisions were intended to do, said the House committee in its majority report, "is to put a stop to strikes that paralyze the economy of our country...."
>
> The Taft bill [in the Senate]...rejected the House idea of outlawing industry-wide or area-wide bargaining. Senator Ball and others offered an amendment to the Taft bill which was generally consistent with the House approach although differing in method....
>
> The Ball amendment was bitterly debated on the Senate floor. On May 7 it was defeated by one vote, 44 to 43.[9]

Although the Hartley bill's provision was dropped in the Senate-House conference that shaped the final act, it is clear that in 1947 Congress came within a one-vote whisker of radically altering the structure of collective bargaining—and, it was hoped, the pattern of strike activity—in this country.

Many similar proposals have been made over the years, and all raise one of the basic problems of strike control in the thorniest fashion possible. If there must be government intervention in labor disputes, everyone would prefer a technique that does not "unfairly" tip the balance of bargaining power toward either labor or management. But because no one can measure bargaining power with any accuracy, we have seen that the conventional strike controls, such as seizure or even the statutory strike, can never guarantee their effects on the balance of power in even one union-management relationship at one point in time. The mind therefore boggles at the enormity of any attempt to determine the "fair" balance of power in *all* union-management relationships for years to come—and yet that is the task facing anyone who sets out to alter the structure of bargaining by a law such as the Hartley proposal.

To take one of the obvious targets of these proposals, it is by no means settled that the steel industry's frequent and lengthy strikes are evidence of too much union power. It can as plausibly be argued that these strikes reflect a power relationship *too evenly balanced,* in the sense that neither party

---

[9]Frank M. Kleiler, "A Legislative History of the National Emergency Provisions" in I. Bernstein, H. L. Enarson, and R. W. Fleming, eds., *Emergency Disputes and National Policy* (New York: Harper, 1955), p. 104.

feels the need to capitulate before the strike deadline and both are so strong that they can weather shutdowns lasting several months. If the latter interpretation happens to be correct, the equitable way to decentralize the industry's bargaining structure would seem to require dismantling the large steel corporations as well as the steel union (unless one frankly wants management to be left with the upper hand). Proposals to crack down simultaneously on big unions and big business have in fact been made at one time or another, but they have predictably generated little enthusiasm in Congress, let alone in labor and employer circles.

On the other hand, assume that in fact the Steelworkers' union does have more power than the steel companies today. The problem now becomes one of how to scale down union power to approximate the strength of each of the 250-plus firms in basic steel or, at least, to equalize the parties' power in each of the 10 largest firms which dominate that industry. If the Hartley bill had said that each union was limited to one *plant*—so that the workers in one U. S. Steel location could not join in the same union with other employees of this giant corporation—that would obviously have stacked the bargaining deck in favor of management. The bill instead provided that each union would be limited to one *company* in industries like steel, so that up to about 250 unions could replace the one union now "monopolizing" steel labor. Some or all of these unions could apparently take joint bargaining action, provided that each union agreed to do so voluntarily and not at the dictation of a national union. In the rather ambiguous words of its sponsors, "The language of the bill does not forbid employees of competing employers to strike at the same time. It forbids their doing so collusively."[10]

What would have been the net effect of this radical change? There are nearly as many answers to that question as there are

[10]"House Report No. 245 on H.R. 3020" in National Labor Relations Board, *Legislative History of the Labor-Management Relations Act, 1947* (Washington, GPO, 1948), vol. 1, p. 315. Also see *ibid.*, pp. 327, 347, 352.

labor experts (which is another suggestive measure of how much we really know about this critical field). The backers of the Hartley bill naturally believed that it would have produced a more equitable distribution of power throughout an industry like steel, with each of the large companies still faced with a union representing its many thousands of workers, small companies facing only small unions, and the chances nil of all these unions striking at the same time for the same demands. On the other hand, most unionists would consider it self-evident that replacing one union with up to 250 unions is throwing the game to management in nearly any industry, and particularly in one with some of the largest corporations in the world and a long history of parallel employer action on both prices and wages.

Other critics suggest that such a structural change might well have produced even worse labor relations in steel, as each of the new unions strove to do better than its "competitor" unions in other companies. When one union represents an industry's entire labor force, runs this argument, the internal political pressures on its leaders impel them to press for "equal pay for equal work" in all companies; when several unions represent workers in the same industry, however, the political pressures frequently flow the other way and each union leader may have to prove himself by trying to deliver more than the leader next door. This, for example, is a frequent complaint of employers in the printing, construction, railroad, and maritime industries, in each of which there are several unions skilled in the arts of whipsawing and leapfrogging. Instead of enduring one do-or-die strike crisis every three years or so, basic steel might therefore have found itself in constant turmoil as first one major contract expired and then another, and union rivalry triggered a chain of company-by-company strikes with a cumulative impact perhaps as great as an industry-wide shutdown.

Finally, to compound the confusion, some critics of proposals such as the Hartley bill assert that it would have changed nothing at all in the basic industries. In steel, for example, it would take "non-collusive" stoppages in only the four largest firms to shut down over 50 percent of the industry's capacity, and strikes in the top ten firms would close down 80 percent of the industry. Nor could the government have proved collusion among the leading steel unions when they struck simultaneously for identical demands, any more than it can now prove collusion among the leading steel firms when their prices magically change at the same time and in precisely the same amount.

The provision in the Hartley bill to permit multiemployer bargaining among small firms within a 50-mile radius also poses several intriguing problems, but they will not be pursued here. Enough has been said, it is hoped, to make one essential point about proposals to narrow the bargaining unit as a method of preventing emergency strikes: they are *not* as radically different from conventional strike controls as either their critics or admirers often assume. Both types of proposals call for the use of government coercion of labor and management to protect the public against certain strikes, while attempting at the same time to preserve as much private bargaining as possible; both have enforcement problems and are unable to guarantee the elimination of emergency strikes—and, perhaps most critical, neither is able to guarantee an equitable impact on the power relationship between labor and management.

There is, however, one very important difference between the proposals to ban industry-wide bargaining and those strike controls such as seizure and the injunction. The former type of proposal clearly would affect far more bargaining relationships far more permanently than the conventional controls. If Congress continues to be handed ticking bombs such as the railroad and airlines disputes of the 1963–1967 period, its members may welcome the appealing logic of eliminating the big strike by eliminating the big bargaining unit. But, until that time, Congress may be restrained, not only by the strong opposition to this proposal from union leaders and most

117

neutral experts, but also by the sobering thought that writing such a law demands a judgment about the balance of power in *most* bargaining relationships that few can confidently make about even a single relationship.

Partial Operation

Partial operation appears to offer a far simpler route to the emergency strike objectives sought by the structural proposals just described. Instead of revamping the structure of *bargaining* throughout the entire country, why not alter the structure of just a few *strikes* affecting the entire country? Everyone agrees that "small" strikes can be tolerated in steel and longshoring and railroads and, in fact, in every private industry in peacetime. So, runs this argument, the best solution to an emergency dispute is for the government to intervene only enough to obtain the necessary minimum of goods or services—through a limited injunction, for example—and to permit labor and management to continue bargaining under the pressures of a partial stoppage.

We have seen that this technique has been proposed for voluntary adoption by the parties and is part of the Javits' seizure proposal. It has also been part of a Massachusetts law since 1947, was endorsed in passing by President Kennedy's tripartite Advisory Committee on Labor-Management Policy, and has been praised by various neutrals.[11]

In fact, nearly everyone seems to favor partial operation in principle but does little about it in practice. In the Livernash study of steel disputes described in Chapter II, for example, mediation and partial operation (to satisfy defense requirements) were the only modes of government intervention to receive a favorable review. Yet, in its 317 pages, this study devoted only one paragraph to the feasibility of partial opera-

---

[11]Shultz, pp. 362–364, 368; *Free and Responsible Collective Bargaining and Industrial Peace*, p. 5; John Perry Horlacher, "A Political Science View of National Emergency Disputes" in *The Annals* of the American Academy of Political and Social Science, vol. 333, January 1961, pp. 94–95.

tion, which said helpfully that there were lots of problems to this approach but a special study (not published) showed that some of these problems could be solved and everyone ought to get busy on the others![12] And in the 1967 shopcraft dispute, the rail unions tried to stave off compulsory arbitration by repeatedly offering to cooperate in moving defense and other critical goods during a strike, but both management and the Administration turned down the offer as impractical and Congress did not pursue it further.[13]

It is easy to discern some of the problems facing this approach. "Part of the difficulty, of course, inheres in the problem of defining a national emergency. A vague concept will not do as a basis for saying what steel production is necessary to prevent the threatened emergency from developing."[14] Even if the parties and the government surmount that hurdle, however, who is to decide *which* companies and workers shall supply the agreed-upon portion of the industry's normal output? For a company, this decision might mean either a decrease or an increase in the losses imposed by a strike, for in some circumstances a company can incur greater costs at a low level of operation than during a complete shutdown.[15] For union members, the decision can mean that some receive full wages while others receive only strike benefits (which are seldom as lavish as many people assume).

Granting these and other difficulties, it is still surprising

[12]U. S. Department of Labor, *Collective Bargaining in the Basic Steel Industry* (Washington: GPO, 1961), p. 48. Also see the brief references to partial operation on p. 18 (one of the nine major conclusions of the entire study) and p. 224 (one sentence out of a chapter devoted to appraising intervention techniques).

[13]See, for example, Bureau of National Affairs, *Daily Labor Report*, May 12, 1967, no. 93, pp. G-1, 2.

[14]Horlacher, p. 95.

[15]In the 1967 shopcraft dispute, the Secretary of Transportation was said to have "estimated the railroads' net loss from a total shutdown would be $31 million a week; from 10 percent operation, $39 million a week; and from 50 percent operation, $13 million a week." Bureau of National Affairs, *Daily Labor Report*, Sept. 21, 1967, no. 184, p. D-4.

that so little systematic attention has been given to a strike control that wins so much approval in principle and has frequently been adopted in practice with little fanfare or furor. Pending the appearance of that definitive work on the subject which everyone would welcome, this study can only echo many others in agreeing that partial operation is certainly a promising idea and in hoping that somebody will someday explore its promise.

Substituting Private for Public Controls

One of the newest proposals on this subject is one which aims to encourage the development of private dispute-settlement machinery by offering an exemption from current strike legislation to those industries that voluntarily adopt adequate private procedures for resolving their impasses.[16] Reportedly endorsed by President Johnson's task force on emergency disputes, this plan attempts to meet the criticism that no single statutory control fits all industries equally well; offers the negotiators in critical industries, who deplore but must now expect government intervention, the opportunity to prevent Washington from "meddling" in their bargaining; and can cite as precedent an effective provision in the Taft-Hartley Act that in 1947 gave the construction industry a similar choice between settling its jurisdictional disputes by some private procedure or having them settled by the National Labor Relations Board.

In industries subject to the Taft-Hartley Act, however, the parties must know that they already have this option open to them. If labor and management in the steel industry agreed to use voluntary arbitration in the event of an impasse, as was vainly proposed in late 1967, there would obviously be no strike to provoke application of Taft-Hartley. Of course, the inducement to adopt private controls could be made stronger by making the existing public controls far more distasteful,

---

[16]Bureau of National Affairs, *Daily Labor Report*, Jan. 20, 1967, no. 14, pp. A-6, 7.

an alternative which would make this proposal simply a variation of the arsenal-of-weapons approach. Finally, in the two industries subject to the Railway Labor Act, voluntary arbitration is now provided as an alternative to the appointment of an emergency board, and it is regularly spurned by labor in critical disputes. In addition, management in the railroad industry has apparently gone so far in accepting the inevitability and desirability of compulsory arbitration that it is most unlikely that these parties could agree on a private alternative to the existing statutory controls.

Conclusions

It must now be clear that one of the easiest parlor games imaginable is puncturing other people's ideas for handling emergency strikes. There is a wide choice of targets, from presidents to professors, and anyone can score a hit with a simple question or two.

Needless to say, that was not the purpose of these last two chapters. It may be recalled that previous chapters documented a widespread dissatisfaction over the postwar years with the emergency strike provisions of both the Taft-Hartley and Railway Labor Acts. Laymen and experts, Republicans and Democrats, labor and management—all, for varying reasons, seemed to want a new strike policy, and yet the provisions in question withstood every attack and in 1968 are precisely the same as they were in 1947. A major reason for their remarkable endurance, this chapter has argued, is the great difficulty of demonstrating that some other strike policy would be much better than the laws now on the books—not because the existing controls are so good, but because our tests of performance in this field are so bad.

Chapter III showed how difficult it is to assess the emergency provisions of the Railway Labor and Taft-Hartley Acts, even with the many facts available on their performance since 1926 and 1947, respectively. Were they applied only to "true" emergencies? What would have happened if they had been applied more sparingly or with fewer presidential attempts to sidestep or improve upon them? No one knows for certain, but the last two chapters showed there is even less certainty about what would happen if some other strike policy were adopted tomorrow.

The case for free collective bargaining, for example, is certainly appealing in many respects, but we have seen that few chief executives have cared to put it to the ultimate test when faced with a major stoppage. Two apparent exceptions were the 1959 steel strike, which was permitted to continue for nearly four months, and the 1967–1968 copper strike, which lasted eight months without provoking formal sanctions. It is true that neither of these massive shutdowns produced a national catastrophe, but it is also true that the federal government eventually intervened in both—applying in each case that curious blend of voluntarism and coercion known as White House-level "mediation," and adding a Taft-Hartley injunction in the steel case. Thus, no one really knows what would happen if existing strike controls were repealed and the President and the Congress, for the first time in nearly a century, resolutely followed a hands-off policy toward all labor disputes. To those who fear the worst, this uncertainty is hardly reassuring.

On the other hand, those who urge a switch to another type of strike control—compulsory arbitration, seizure, the statutory strike, or the arsenal-of-weapons approach—are always challenged on the enforceability and equity of their proposals. On the first point, there is no compelling evidence that these other controls would win any more (or less) compliance from labor and management than the existing laws have achieved, so why change for this reason? As for equity, neither Taft-Hartley nor the Railway Labor Act can assure a fair settlement or an even-handed impact on the bargaining power of the private parties—but neither can any other strike control, given our inability to define a "fair settlement" or to measure "bargaining power" with any precision.

The Search for a Better Strike Policy

Finally, the proposal to ban industry-wide bargaining trips over the same obstacle. Billed as an escape from the hazards of conventional strike controls, this proposal can require the most hazardous guesswork of any strike policy: predicting how a ceiling on bargaining units will affect the balance of power in nearly all union-management relationships, not just the few at which other controls are aimed.

Paradoxically, then, nearly *any* of the strike controls described in this chapter might have endured over the postwar period as tenaciously as the 80-day injunction of Taft-Hartley and the emergency board procedures of the Railway Labor Act. Once a particular control becomes the law of the land, the burden of proof rests heavily on those who argue for a change, and in this field there are very few standards of "proof" to which the critics can appeal. As one more example, if Congress in 1947 had adopted some other strike control which had then compiled a mixed record over the next twenty years, imagine how difficult it would be today to argue for a change to such a one-sided and inconclusive technique as an 80-day injunction!

No one, of course, ever has perfect knowledge about any social or political problem. On the subject of emergency strikes, however, the imperfections in our knowledge are embarrassingly numerous and fundamental: whether there even *is* a strike problem that needs a solution, whether the solutions tried during the past several years have worked reasonably well or have made matters worse, and whether some other solution would have worked any better over the same period. If there is this little consensus on the past record of strike policy, on which everyone has the benefit of hindsight, small wonder that there exists a paralyzing disagreement over the course that strike policy should follow in the future.

VI

Some Opinions and Proposals

IF ANY READER EXPECTS TO FIND "the answer" to emergency strikes in this final chapter, he should go to the foot of the class. If, instead, the reader has been reduced to a state of healthy confusion, seeing numerous perils lurking in *every* possible strike policy, he may now count himself an expert on this subject. In fact, this study will have made its major point if the following opinions of its author are viewed with a balance of tolerance and skepticism.

First, is there really an "emergency strike problem" at all? On this question, it is hard to escape the conclusion that public opinion has been ahead of expert opinion through much of the postwar period. For too long, the debate among the professionals over this issue has turned on the unfortunate wording of the Taft-Hartley Act, which authorizes government intervention only in strikes that are "national emergencies" that "imperil the national health or safety." Taken literally, these phrases permit intervention only in strikes that threaten misery and devastation on a scale unknown in this country except during major wars and depressions. Presumably a general strike would qualify as a true "national emergency," if it were like the 1968 upheaval in France when nearly half of that country's entire labor force walked out (or sat in) for more than two weeks. Even then, no one starved because of that strike nor did the French economy collapse.

Few critics of strike controls are quite that literal in defining "national emergencies," but many judge this type of intervention by standards that would be considered harsh if applied to other labor legislation. Consider, for example, the laws that now fix minimum wages, provide pensions and unemployment insurance, and forbid employers to discriminate against Negroes and union members. Who could prove that any of these laws is necessary to preserve the national health or safety from imminent peril? Indeed, given nearly any social problem but strikes, who would even advance such a standard today as the sole justification for government intervention?

It would therefore be a small step forward if serious discussions of this subject avoided the very phrase, "national emergency strikes," and used some substitute term such as "critical strikes" or "strikes seriously affecting the national welfare." Any such terms are fearfully ambiguous, but that is just the point: in the real world, the moment at which the government should intervene in a strike *is* uncertain and indefinable. The criterion of "national emergency" appears comfortingly precise, but no Administration would or should remain passive until a strike has brought the nation to the brink of a genuine emergency. For this reason, the interventionists have interpreted "national emergency" so loosely as to rob the phrase of its intrinsic meaning, while their critics have interpreted it so literally as to rob the phrase of any utility.

Let us admit that Congress blundered in writing this phrase into law, and then drop once and for all the pretense that there are only two kinds of strikes: those in which the government should do nothing and those once-in-a-lifetime cataclysms in which the government may do anything. The hard problems of strike policy fall squarely between those extremes, where it is perfectly reasonable for the public to expect its elected officials to do something about "serious" labor disputes that are neither

Some Opinions and Proposals

trivial nor catastrophic in their impact on third parties. Adopting some other criterion as vague as "the public interest" or "national welfare" obviously would *not* answer the critical questions of when and how the government should step into a particular work stoppage. Such a change might, however, pose these questions more honestly than the scare term of "national emergency."

As a second and corollary conclusion, there is no escaping the need for executive discretion in triggering any strike control so far devised. Even though Congress laid down a stringent definition of emergency disputes in the Taft-Hartley Act, for example, no one has yet prevented a President from invoking that law whenever he chose or has forced a President to use it when he chose not to. In fact, this law would probably have been used no differently over the past twenty-one years if it had been written vaguely to apply to something like "strikes affecting the public interest" instead of trying to pinpoint those which "imperil the national health or safety."

Of course, if there were some yardstick for quickly and reliably measuring a strike's actual impact (or, even better, its potential impact if allowed to continue), Congress could conceivably limit presidential discretion by designating "impact scores" that would bar or require intervention. As the evidence in Chapter II makes plain, however, we are light-years away from devising any such magic measure.

One improvement in the crude measures now used could be contributed by an agency like the United States Employment Service, if it were directed to make systematic assessments of the secondary unemployment caused by a major strike, to replace the haphazard assessments now made by newspaper reporters. As suggested by the Chamberlain-Schilling and New York subway studies described in Chapter II, many strikes probably damage third parties far less in their role as consumers than in their role as producers. It is easy to shrug off a strike that simply holds up the delivery of Cadillacs or color television sets for a few weeks, but surely it is more than a mere inconvenience if for weeks the same strike cuts off the income of thousands of workers and employers not involved in the dispute.

But even if accurate information were available on that neglected type of strike effect, the basic problem would remain. As a guide to strike policy, it is useless to counsel "no intervention except in national emergencies," and we have no objective way of determining when the government should intervene short of a state of emergency. Any strike policy that aims to provide "some but not too much" intervention must therefore rely upon executive discretion. This in turn means that the decision to intervene or not will in some measure always be a political decision—but who can pretend to have the hard facts necessary to eliminate political judgment from the field of strike policy?

A third element to recognize in fashioning a viable strike policy is that ultimate solutions are fortunately rare in a free society. John Dunlop has made this point very well:

> There can be no final resort to end emergency disputes. But there is also no way convincingly to still the insistent question: then what? If mediation fails, then what? If fact-finding and recommendations do not produce settlement, then what? If seizure and injunction fail, then what? If the use of the armed forces or putting workers in the militia fail, then what? If you put the leaders in jail and there is still no settlement, then what? The quest for the end of this road is a dangerous illusion.[1]

This search for certainty is dangerous, of course, because it inevitably leads to crippling the liberties of the many in an attempt to guarantee the compliance of the few. The evidence is perfectly clear that *American unions and employers will comply with most strike controls most of the time, but that every control will sooner or later be violated by someone.*

Because no strike law can guarantee to end every strike to which it is applied, some "doves" on this subject conclude

---

[1]John T. Dunlop, "The Settlement of Emergency Disputes," *Proceedings of Fifth Annual Meeting of Industrial Relations Research Association, Dec. 1952* (Madison, Wis.: IRRA, 1953), p. 118.

Some Opinions and Proposals

that all such laws are futile or worse—a curious logic that is seldom applied to the few thousand other laws that do not guarantee perfect compliance. By much the same reasoning, some "hawks" conclude that the only answer to the strike problem is to obliterate union power through harsher methods than conventional strike controls. But surely the most sensible conclusion is that there is just no point in searching for a public policy that is so punitive (or equitable or clever) that it will solve the strike problem with more finality than we have achieved in tackling any other social problem. If this suggests that the hawks on this subject should abandon their dreams of filling the jails with strikers, it also suggests that the doves should drop their pose that any imperfect strike control is worse than no control at all.

Time for a Change

The above are surely mild conclusions: that society has a legitimate interest in curbing the few strikes that may have a serious effect on third parties; that there is no objective measure for determining when intervention is warranted in a particular stoppage, so this decision must continue to be a matter of judgment; and that no strike control can guarantee a just and peaceful solution to every major dispute. If these opinions are accepted, however, they lead to the further conclusion that we should scrap the strike laws now on the books and adopt in their place one of the several more imaginative policies that are readily available.

The statutory strike particularly deserves far more consideration than it has received. More than any other proposal, it addresses itself squarely to the three goals of an ideal strike control: continued operation for the protection of third-party interests; an even-handed impact of government on the power relationship of labor and management; and a strong inducement for the private parties to settle their dispute by themselves. The statutory strike meets none of these goals completely, of course, for its central feature—the "strike tax" imposed on both parties—cannot possibly be precise in its attempt to apply equal and sufficient pressure to induce a voluntary settlement. What its critics overlook, however, is that *all* strike controls impinge on the parties' power relationship and few even attempt to do so equitably.

If the statutory strike is too candid in exposing the heart of the strike control problem (or, more politely, too ambitious to be practical at this time), there are other policies that still would be more effective or more equitable than existing controls. The suggested new approaches to compulsory arbitration, for example, appear very promising. If labor and management knew that a failure to settle would mean incurring very high "arbitration fees" (actually a variation of the statutory strike), or even better that an arbitrator would be required to choose the deadline position of one party or the other, this prospect should greatly reduce the danger of sham bargaining that has always plagued the idea of compulsory arbitration.

Or more politically palatable, and certainly worth more than the lip service it usually receives, is the proposal for partial operation as a method for meeting the most critical needs of the public while permitting the private bargaining process to continue in a smaller arena. In principle, at least, this technique is highly flexible, for it could be employed either on its own (at the request of the President) or to make other controls more palatable, such as seizure (as in the Javits' bill) or the injunction or even the statutory strike. Perhaps it would prove to be an administrative nightmare, but at the very least it should be included in any arsenal-of-weapons proposal and its possibilities examined by Congress or some enterprising expert.

As for the arsenal of weapons, some of its popularity may well be due to the fact that it creates the illusion of change while frequently offering little that is new in substance. Some arsenals are better stocked than others, however, so even though the uncertainty thesis has been oversold this approach could still be valuable as a testing ground for promising ideas. This would require a Congress willing to grant a President such

Some Opinions and Proposals

options as partial operation, the statutory strike, and the new versions of compulsory arbitration (together with the usual options of fact finding, injunction, and the like), and it would also require a President with the courage to gamble occasionally on an untried weapon in a major dispute. If this unlikely combination were ever to occur, then the arsenal-of-weapons approach could provide a vehicle for improving strike policy without having to risk everything on a promising but untried idea.

Thus, there is no shortage of ways to improve federal policy governing critical strikes. The problem is how to induce Congress to adopt one or the other of these improvements, given the obstacles of the offsetting political power of labor and management and the difficulty of "proving" much of anything in this field. The latter obstacle would shrink considerably, however, if only more people would frankly acknowledge its existence—acknowledge, for example, that the "national emergency" test is nearly useless; that there is no precise measure of bargaining power or strike impact or equity in labor disputes; and in other ways admit that we must choose among uncertain and imperfect remedies in this field, as we do in all other areas of public policy. If the strike problem were approached with more tolerance and candor, we would see that the emergency provisions of the Taft-Hartley and Railway Labor Acts, while better than most of their critics assert, are not as effective or equitable as any of the policies above would probably be.

A Postscript

Throughout this study, it has been assumed that certain strikes are critical solely because of their effect on the flow of goods and services to consumers or the flow of income to workers and employers outside the struck units. For this and other reasons, it has also been assumed that the *content* of an agreement in a critical dispute is of far less importance than that the *method* of agreement be relatively peaceful and, to the extent possible, voluntary. Today, these orthodox assumptions are

131

under severe challenge from those who view collective bargaining as a major contributor to the twin problems of inflation and unemployment.

The problems surrounding the wage-price-employment relationship are obviously too complex to be described here in any detail. Very briefly, everyone is in favor of full employment, stable prices, and a minimum of economic controls, but no modern economy has yet achieved all three of these goals simultaneously. As the goal of full employment is approached, any number of forces may trigger a wage-price spiral which, once begun, is impossible to kill off painlessly. To keep ahead of rising prices, workers understandably demand higher wage increases and can get them when labor markets are tight and unions are strong. To keep ahead of rising costs, employers understandably demand higher prices from consumers and can get them when product markets are tight and corporations are strong—which of course sets off further demands for higher wages and prices, and the process may repeat itself over and over, with no one the villain and yet everyone a victim.

At this point, society faces a dismal choice of remedies: to accept inflation, which no one wants; or to chill the economy with a strong dose of unemployment, which no one wants; or to slap on wage and price controls, which no one wants; or to break up big unions or big companies, which many people want but will not get, for a variety of good and bad reasons.

All of this has several implications for the problem of strike policy. At the very least, we should resign ourselves to the fact that this problem is going to be with us for as long as we can foresee. In the 1940–1955 period, there was a hope that the strike problem would wither away as collective bargaining matured and we moved out of the turbulence of wartime controls and postwar inflation. In the recession years of the late 1950's and early 1960's, the tough disputes all seemed to spring from technological change and shrinking job opportunities, and the basic solution was obviously full employment.

Some Opinions and Proposals

In the mid-1960's, we closed in on full employment but strikes and intervention both increased in frequency, presumably because of Vietnam and inflation.

Surely we should begin to suspect that the critical strike is just not going to fade away. Even if peace should break out tomorrow, the evidence suggests that in periods of full employment there will be a high level of strike activity and the constant threat of a wage-price spiral, and in recession years there will be fewer strikes but more that are long and hard-fought because dwindling jobs and profits are at stake.

This in turn suggests that in good years the government will be increasingly concerned with the *content* of a strike settlement, as it obviously has been since the formulation of the wage and price guideposts in 1962.[2] In some disputes, this concern might paradoxically lead to a greater toleration of strikes by public officials, if they believed that this was the only way for an employer to beat back an excessive wage demand. In other cases, however, there might be even less patience with strikes, if an employer were suspected of welcoming a stoppage as an excuse for a price increase planned well before the strike. Also, as if we did not have enough trouble measuring strike effects, there is now an increasing concern with the impact of certain strikes on the rate of inventory accumulation in the economy and on the nation's balance of payments.

And finally, if the wage-price problem continues to defy other solutions, we may well see intervention in negotiations that threaten no strike whatever. The guidepost policy, for

[2] Among neutral experts and labor and management officials, the reaction to the guideposts often bore a fascinating similarity to earlier reactions to strike controls. Both types of government action were predictably denounced as unwarranted meddling in private decisions and as biased toward either labor or management, but both were also criticized for being too weak to have any effect and too strong to permit free markets to operate normally, which is quite a trick. Also, both attracted more than their share of critics who seldom bothered to offer anything better as a solution to the problems at hand.

133

example, assumes that the wage and price decisions made in certain basic and highly visible sectors of the economy will influence the level of all wages and prices, both directly and as a model for pattern followers in other industries. If this is true, an inflationary settlement in a key industry becomes a cause of concern whether it is reached with or without benefit of a strike. At that point, the question of what constitutes an "emergency strike" justifying government intervention—a question never answered adequately in over twenty years of debate—will have been transformed into the even stickier question of what constitutes a "critical negotiation."

In the midst of all this gloom and doom, there remains one ray of hope: on the subjects of collective bargaining and government intervention, economists are born pessimists with a long list of bad predictions to their credit. It must be hoped that they are wrong again today, for we have seen that strike policy has more than enough hazards to surmount without taking on any responsibility for price stability and full employment. Unfortunately, candor requires the conclusion that the strike problem in the United States is probably going to get worse, because of the wage-price issue, long before it gets any better.